T0201537

"*Rediscovering Christmas* reveals how a story set in Bethlehem two thousand years ago is still brimming with fresh meaning and purpose. AJ Sherrill introduces you to a motley crew of characters who will help you experience the Christmas season and story in a more contextual, personal, and deeply profound way. The writing is thoughtful, inspiring, accessible, and it will help prepare your heart and soul for all the Christmas season has to offer."

—STEVE CARTER, pastor and author of
Grieve, Breathe, Receive

"By exploring the well-known characters of the first Advent in depth, I was drawn into their stories and discovered my own vulnerabilities, aspirations, and desires mirrored in them. Having experienced this book, I anticipate Christmas with a fresh outlook on its potential for spiritual rejuvenation and healing in my personal journey."

—LIBBY VANSOLKEMA, president of Ancient Paths Study
Tours and creative resource director at
Crossroads Bible Church

Rediscovering Christmas

REDISCOVERING CHRISTMAS

Surprising Insights into the Story

You Thought You Knew

✳

AJ SHERRILL

Foreword by Rich Villodas

WaterBrook

Published in the United States by WaterBrook, an imprint of Random House, a division of Penguin Random House LLC.

WATERBROOK and colophon are registered trademarks of Penguin Random House LLC.

Photo on page 80: Isenheim Altarpiece (first view) by Matthias Grünewald and Nikolaus Hagenauer, c. 1512–1516. Unterlinden Museum, Colmar, France. Martyrdom of Saint Sebastian; Crucifixion; Saint Anthony the Great.

LIBRARY OF CONGRESS CATALOGING-IN-PUBLICATION DATA
Names: Sherill, AJ, author.
Title: Rediscovering Christmas : surprising insights into the story you thought you knew / AJ Sherill.
Description: First edition. | Colorado Springs : WaterBrook, [2024] | Includes bibliographical references.
Identifiers: LCCN 2024018793 | ISBN 9780593445532 (hardcover) | ISBN 9780593445549 (ebook)
Subjects: LCSH: Christmas—Biblical teaching. | Jesus Christ—Nativity—Biblical teaching. | Bible stories.
Classification: LCC BT315.3 .S48 2024 | DDC 242/.335—dc23/eng/20240606
LC record available at https://lccn.loc.gov/2024018793

Printed in the United States of America on acid-free paper

waterbrookmultnomah.com

2 4 6 8 9 7 5 3 1

First Edition

Book design by Virginia Norey

Most WaterBrook books are available at special quantity discounts for bulk purchase for premiums, fundraising, and corporate and educational needs by organizations, churches, and businesses. Special books or book excerpts also can be created to fit specific needs. For details, contact specialmarketscms@penguinrandomhouse.com.

Foreword

I've lived in New York City my entire life. I know this place.
I love this place. It's home. But something happened in 2018
that opened my eyes to things I'd never seen or knew. What
happened? I went on a tour.

Money was tight that year, so we couldn't take a trip to
another part of the country. We decided instead to see our
beloved city again for the first time. We took in sights from
the observation deck at the Empire State Building. We visited museums we'd never heard of before. We found restaurants and neighborhoods that had been there a long time but
were new to us. We became tourists in our own backyard.

That summer, I discovered an important truth: *Familiarity has a way of eliminating wonder.* This is essentially how I
describe my experience of reading the book in your hands.
Christmas is all too familiar for most of us. We have lived
here a long time. We know this season. We love this season.
We feel at home in it. But what if I told you there's more? So
much more.

Sometimes, to truly see and know what's in front of us
requires a tour—and a trustworthy tour guide. That's exactly what you're in for with AJ Sherrill and *Rediscovering
Christmas.* AJ does something in this book that few can. He

integrates history, culture, theology, and spiritual formation in an accessible, winsome, and soul-inspiring way.

This book will challenge the assumptions you have about Christmas and (re)introduce you to the Advent season that precedes it. This book will unveil truths about history and culture that will help you better understand the story we've become so familiar with. Through these pages, you will see the wide-ranging connections in Scripture that help make better sense of the sweeping big story of Christmas.

And not only that, but AJ will also help you establish spiritual practices that can renew your heart and kindle love for God, which might be the best Christmas gift you can receive.

In one of the chapters in this book, AJ notes that we lose our ability to spiritually see as we age. I couldn't agree more, especially with regard to Christmas. But that can change today.

Christmas is a vast city. Within it are places we've never ventured. Streets we've not walked on. Sights we haven't taken in. Experiences we haven't enjoyed. But thankfully, we have an expert guide in AJ and a gracious king in Jesus.

I'm excited for you to rediscover Christmas.

—RICH VILLODAS, lead pastor of New Life Fellowship and author of *The Deeply Formed Life, Good and Beautiful and Kind,* and *The Narrow Path*

Contents

RE-*TEL*-LING CHRISTMAS

HAVE YOU EVER HEARD OF A TEL? AND, NO, *TEL* IS not misspelled. A tell in middle school is a snitch who informs the teacher of another student's misbehavior. That is not the word I am referring to. A tell in poker is when a person's body language gives away their hand. That, also, is not what I am referring to. A tel is a hill of civilization that has been built upon repeatedly over a long period of time. Jerusalem is a tel. Much of the Holy Land is a tel. You've probably heard of the city Tel Aviv. *Tel* means "hill" and *Aviv* means "spring." If you dig down through the layers of time, you will find cultures and civilizations buried like hidden treasure. My friend Libby likens a tel to children building with Legos. Imagine one child comes along and builds a foundation with them. Then another child later comes along and builds upon the first child's efforts. Multiply that by ten other kids in succession thereafter. That's what a tel is like. It's a hill full of culture.

Would you believe that some tels in the Near East are more than twenty layers of civilization? That's deep! All those layers make it challenging to know what's underneath. What does this have to do with Christmas? Well, metaphorically speaking, Christmas is a tel. Over the centuries, various cultures have taken the story and overlain their own traditions. Whereas that is often personal and beautiful, the original meaning can become obscured like in the game of telephone, where we whisper a word to our neighbor and ask them to pass it on. This book is an attempt to unearth and explore the original meaning of Christmas. As you dig underneath the traditions built up along the way, new meaning can be discovered and fresh faith kindled. Consider the tel of Christmas:

Sometimes meaning gets buried. Think about the layers of Christmas culture that can make it difficult to uncover the original story. The surface layer most evident in culture today is the one that elicits thoughts of Aunt Sally's fruit-cake, bargain chasing, and the consumerist myth of Santa Claus prompting children to believe that the presents under the tree are the fruits of good behavior. This book is an invitation to dig beneath the layers of the Christmas tel.

Come with me.

As you rediscover Christmas, you will find your heart once again opening to the wider field of God's love, empowering you to participate in the new creation story launched at Christmas and extending far beyond December 25 into the rest of the year.

The story of Christmas centers on God *with* us. And this means that God always and forever refuses to be God *without* us. The story is true!

Introduction

WHAT IS CHRISTMAS ABOUT? IMAGINE YOU CAN USE only one word to answer that question. What would you write? Here is a line for you: _____.

Maybe you wrote *Jesus* or *Immanuel.* Or maybe for you Christmas is the season of *joy* or *hope* or *gifts.* Perhaps your life experience has led you to dread it because of family drama, holiday stress, or endless fruitcake. One would rightly suggest that Christmas has become about any of those words. But in recent years, I've added a new word to my list, which I am happy to share with you in a moment.

But first consider a (very big) number: 80,213,066.

Spelled out, that's eighty million, two hundred thirteen thousand, sixty-six. That's a lot. So, what does Christmas Day have to do with that number?

Maybe it's the number of times you've watched the film *A Christmas Story.*

Maybe it's the number of times you've decided not to watch the film *A Christmas Story*.

Maybe it's the number of Christmas songs played on your local radio between Thanksgiving and New Year's.

This number—80,213,066—is the total amount of dollars that came through the movie-theater box office on Christmas Day 2017, which, at first glance, isn't that fascinating.[1] But a more interesting question to consider is, *Why would all that money spill into Hollywood on a religious holiday?* It turns out there are good reasons people like to watch movies on Christmas Day.

Deep within each of us is a longing to hear a good story. And in the season of Christmas, the Gospels tell the greatest story in the world. But because of overfamiliarity, triviality, and ignorance, we often leave the depths of the Nativity story unexplored, instead settling for cheesy films, shallow Christmas services, and increased consumer spending to define for us the meaning of Christmas. Which leads us back to the opening question: What is Christmas about?

As promised, here is my answer. Christmas, in one word, is about . . . *bread*.

To explain, allow me to tell you a brief story.

The sanctuary filled fast. It was Christmas Eve, and having been a pastor for decades, I was well acquainted with the fun frenzy of the special church service. Whether the people's motives for gathering were that of sacred devotion or religious obligation didn't matter to me. All minds were fixed; hearts were attuned; bodies were attentive to engaging the greatest story ever told. But instead of feeding them the Christmas message they'd heard for decades, I went with a different approach to disrupt familiarity.

Emily Dickinson reminded us to always "tell all the truth but tell it slant."[2] What she meant was that overfamiliarity tends to dull our senses to any given story. Therefore, we must always search for new ways to present old truths. That Christmas Eve, I told the story of the birth of God's Son in a way that was perhaps more "slanted" than the Leaning Tower of Pisa (without compromising or obscuring the truth, of course).

I held up a small box and asked one simple question pertaining to the central message of the Christmas story: "Can anyone guess what lies within?"

Some said a star; others said a manger (it would have been a very small manger). My favorite guess came from a child who shouted out, "Jesus!" Yes, Jesus is the central message of the story, but no, I did not have a tiny Jesus hidden in the box.

After hearing a few more guesses, I opened the box and pulled out a croissant. The gathered crowd oohed and aahed. Hoisting the croissant up high, I pronounced that the Scriptures claim that the central message of the Christmas story is bread! Everyone cheered at the sight of the pastry because, let's be honest, even gluten-free enthusiasts might find it hard to resist the allure of a croissant.

Christmas is about bread. It's hidden in plain sight on the first pages of the New Testament. Think about bread through these three words: *Jesus, Bethlehem,* and *manger.*

Say them aloud:

Jesus . . .

Bethlehem . . .

Manger . . .

As we will see, all three words are related to bread. And connecting the dots will deepen your understanding of the Christmas story.

First, consider the name *Jesus*. In John's gospel, Jesus disclosed his identity through seven "I AM" statements. One of the seven ways Jesus referred to himself was as bread. To his disciples, he said, "I am the *bread* of life" (John 6:35). Those who feast on him will not go hungry. Hold on to that idea.

Next, consider the town of Bethlehem. In Hebrew, *Bethlehem* is a compound word, which simply means the word can be broken down into two separate words. Bethlehem = *bet* + *lechem*. *Bet* means "house," and *lechem* means "bread." Bethlehem, therefore, means "house of bread." Hold on to that idea as well.

Finally, consider the word *manger*. Mangers are not wooden beds filled with pillows in the form of hay. A manger in the time of Jesus was cut from stone and served as a trough to hold feed for animals. In the cold winter months, animals—and mangers—were sometimes placed within the front section of the home. (More on that in a later chapter on the innkeeper, who, incidentally, didn't exist.)

When we put the puzzle pieces together, we see that the New Testament is telling a story about the arrival of a man named *Jesus* (the Bread of Life), who was born in a town called *Bethlehem* (the house of bread) and immediately placed in a *manger* (feeding trough).

So, the Bread of Life . . .

was born in the *house of bread* . . .

and placed in a *feeding trough* . . .

to satisfy the hunger of every human heart.

That is the meaning of Christmas. We must never settle for less.

We don't need new stories from Hollywood on Christmas Day. Instead, we must reclaim the ancient depth and wonder of the Jesus story. Christ, our savior, is the Bread of Life. Let us keep the feast! The coming chapters will help us do that.

WHY THIS BOOK?

Rediscovering Christmas holistically addresses challenges we face this time of year. The core problem is that we feast on cultural stories that fail to satisfy our greatest hunger. Our settling for less depletes our minds, hearts, and bodies.

In what ways do we settle for less?

First, we settle for *sentimental explanations* of the Christmas story. This negatively affects our minds. Many people errantly think they have heard all there is to know about the Nativity account. But that will never be true. The story is gloriously deep, with hidden meaning awaiting discovery. Overfamiliarity with the Scriptures can cause a lack of the curiosity necessary for further biblical discoveries. So, instead of going deeper, many settle for cheap slogans and greeting-card insight. In short, Christmas can become sentimental rather than transformative. When we settle in this way, our minds become dull and bored. But within the Gospels are buried treasures waiting for us to unearth. I'll show you a few in this book. Pastors, priests, and clergy of all kinds must continue to deepen their understanding of Scripture and then teach the church to rekindle lost wonder. The church deserves (and can handle) depth beyond sappy Christmas-card theology and contemporary anecdotes that entertain but do not nourish souls.

Second, we settle for *consumer goods* our culture sells us. The Amazon cart is full, but the human heart is empty. Christmas is not about chasing discounts or consumer debt or maxed-out credit cards. By Christmas Eve, many of us are too emotionally drained to offer much adoration to the Christ child in the manger. We've all seen the cliché commercial played out in the suburban driveway—the ad where the man walks outside to find an overpriced new truck with an oversized bow on the hood. I'm not saying that buying a new car is wrong, but the deeper joy is waiting in the manger, not the driveway. When we settle for consumer joy (which is an illusion), our hearts are robbed of the joy God longs for us to experience.

Third, we settle for a *hurried pace* more in December than during any other month of the year. Our hurried society demands busyness, crowding our calendars with events that wear us down. Our bodies are tired, and we feel it by December 26. We also struggle to experience the true meaning of Christmas when we've spent most of the month running around shopping malls, navigating parking lots, and saying yes to every invitation, well intentioned as we may be. When we settle for a hurried pace, we fail to appreciate the One who came in flesh, taking a body and becoming bread for our sake. You are a powerful person who can say "no thanks" when necessary. Exercise your power this season.

HOW THIS BOOK IS STRUCTURED

Rediscovering Christmas will provide you with fresh, biblical insight to renew your mind, engaging art to reawaken your heart, and practical application to restore your body. This book is divided into two sections, or themes: *Advent,* which teaches us the meaning of waiting; and *Christmas,* which teaches us the meaning of receiving. Each chapter examines a different biblical character (or group of characters) who corresponds to one of the two parts of the book (Advent or Christmas). By looking at ancient context and current culture, I aim to reveal fresh insight into each biblical character in ways you've perhaps never seen or heard. Once we understand a deeper perspective from their stories, we can then apply the lessons of their journeys to our own. These historic characters from the Gospels are meant to serve as close companions to help form us rightly. Every chapter will begin with a Scripture passage. Reading these will help you better digest the chapter contents before ending by viewing a sketch to draw you into deeper reflection and practice.

It's a curious thing that *wonder* and *wander* are so similarly spelled in the English language. What for many began as wonder can easily drift into wander over the years. Wherever you are on your sacred journey, I pray that wonder would mark your days this season.

As a pastor, author, father, friend, and spouse, I needed this book years ago. Therefore, I determined to write it. May you experience God's greatest gift over your life; namely, the gift called Immanuel—God with us. And may you know the meaning of waiting so that you also experience the wonder of receiving. In Christ, our deepest hunger is fully satisfied. So prepare him room and feast on the pages before you.

Part 1

ADVENT

The Gift of Waiting

※

⁎

Advent is not Christmas. It is a time of preparation for Christmas. Little Advent, little Christmas. Great Advent, great Christmas. I'll explain.

Each of the seven characters in part 1 is meant to shape our Advent journey—a journey of patient hope and joyful expectation. Just as those long ago awaited the arrival of the Messiah in the form of a child, we now wait for the arrival of the Messiah in the form of a king. They awaited the Savior's first coming. Now we await the second.

Coming from the Latin word *adventus, Advent* means "arrival." And because the full arrival of God's kingdom is still to come, we find ourselves in a similar place as the ancients: a people in waiting. But Advent isn't that kind of waiting, where apathy, boredom, and despair set in (such as at a doctor's office waiting room). Rather, it's a kind of waiting that knows something significant about where the future is heading and how we may best position our lives for that future while living in the present. So we wait, but we wait with hope.

In the great tradition of the Christian faith, Advent—not January 1—is the beginning of a new year. It (usually) begins on the first Sunday in December and leads us to Christmas Eve.

Properly understood, Advent pushes against singing "Joy to the World" before Christmas Day. Mary had to wait nine months to birth Jesus; therefore, we should be willing to wait one month. In fact, Advent stands in opposition to much of what we experience on the radio and at contemporary evangelical church services. The season of four weeks wants to help us cultivate waiting, hope, and longing. And longing isn't short. Longing literally takes a looooong time or it's not really a longing, is it?

It Starts in the Dark

As the church proclaims the beginning of a new year, one of the gifts of this season is given to people who are sitting in darkness. This darkness may take the form of an unwelcome health diagnosis, financial strain, an end to a relationship, or a crisis of faith. The list goes on. The gift of the season lies in its capacity to make space for people who do not have life all together, wrapped in a bow of joy. The church authentically proclaims that the gospel is for the broken, the outsider, and the wandering soul in search of light. We often want to get to Christmas morning a little too quickly. We yearn to sing "Joy to the World" next to the shepherds and offer gifts of praise to God alongside the Magi. But first we are called to sit with John the Baptist in the dark of the desert. It is there that we get in touch with our great need. It is there that we might learn what our souls really hunger for. And instead of feeding on fillers, we make space for God's presence.

Author Tish Harrison Warren suggested that "Advent is practice in waiting."[1] No wonder Advent is omitted in the church for many people today, as we live in a society that orchestrates life to wait as little as possible. For some, the idea of Advent is trendy. After all, people generally like lighting candles. But the true lived experience of Advent for a month is the opposite of what the digital age affords us. Instead of practicing waiting, we are deeply (mal)formed in habits of immediacy, impatience, and efficiency in today's culture.

Mary, the mother of Jesus, modeled Advent for us. Her Advent—that is, waiting for arrival—was not merely four Sundays but rather nine months. She demonstrated for us what happens inside a person when they create space for something better. In the Advent season, the church, following the liturgical calendar, will often light a candle for the four Sundays before Christmas. These candles follow themes such as hope, peace, joy, and love. As we wait, our hearts yearn to be formed into these themes.

Advent waiting allows God time to do deep work in us. But we must not confuse waiting with an invitation to fall into apathy, laziness, or despair. We wait in hope, expectantly vigilant for God to complete what he has begun. Active waiting is the call of the church.

Firepit Spirituality

Author and pastor Brian Zahnd wrote, "Ours is a secular age. The sacred is pushed to the periphery. To keep the sacred at the center of our lives is a heroic act of defiance."[2] Zahnd was right. To faithfully live into the sacred calendar of the church requires effort. Society discourages waiting and offers devices of all kinds that habituate us into immediacy. Once the Thanksgiving decor is put away, the Christmas tree comes out. The celebration begins! Advent is omitted. We are ready for December 25 before December starts. Resist this urge. There is something waiting for you in the waiting. Guard the sacred as the center. Later, I will make some recommendations as to how you might do that.

Just the other day, I was writing at my friend's farmhouse in the deep forests of South Carolina. As I was attempting to start a fire, the whirling winds frustrated the task, but shielding the embers from the winds allowed the flame to grow. It occurred to me that this is similar to what we face this season. Advent shields us from the hurried and demanding winds of life trying to blow out the flame of God within us. But we must guard that flame of hope, because waiting is difficult. We must shield and protect it, lest it be snuffed out by the demands of immediacy. We are waiting for the Light of the World (see John 1:9), and that light has called us to be a city on a hill (see Matthew 5:14, ESV). The winds of life come in the form of busyness, ennui, consumerism, stress, food preparation, and numerous activities that slowly add up until exhaustion sets in. If you allow them, these winds will smother the flame that burns on Christmas morning.

Maybe the invitation of Advent is to slow down—to say no and be still, lingering in the night without the false light of screens. Maybe it's to turn our hearts upward in worship and to light candles of hope in the comfort of our living rooms.

We wait again with the ancients for the child to be placed in the manger, but we also wait with the church for the return of the King. We wait, therefore, in both directions: past and future. And we do this in the present moment. Just as the arrival eventually came all those years ago, so the arrival will come again when Jesus forever sets up his reign on earth. Isaiah comforts us in our waiting. It is not in vain:

> For to us a child is born,
>> to us a son is given,
>> and the government will be on his shoulders.
> And he will be called
>> Wonderful Counselor, Mighty God,
>> Everlasting Father, Prince of Peace.
>>> (Isaiah 9:6)

Advent Pathway

The seven chapters in the Advent section are meant to support your journey of active waiting. Here are some suggestions, which are invitations, not obligations:

1. Make a schedule to read each of the seven Advent chapters of this book before Christmas. (I recommend reading in the morning, if possible, because

your mind is more alert when you first wake. This is the decision to offer up to God the best of your brain energy each day.)

2. Begin each reading with the lighting of a candle inviting Christ, the Light of the World, who will come to illumine your path.

3. Conclude each chapter by reflecting on the provided sketch for three to five minutes, asking God to fill your imagination with fresh faith and application.

4. Commit to worshipping with a local church body for each of the four weeks in Advent.

5. Resist anything that might dull your senses as you wait for the arrival of true spiritual food (for example, alcohol consumption, excessive Christmas music, and unhealthy foods).

Little Advent, little Christmas. Great Advent, great Christmas!

Be strong, and let your heart take courage,
all you who wait for the Lord!
—Psalm 31:24, esv

1

MARY: PRESENCE

The Practice of Filling the Heart
Luke 1:26–38

EVERY YEAR, CHRISTMAS RETURNS TO US WITH THE rise of consumer sales, various holiday pageants, and endless desserts. Santa, sweaters, and sweet baby Jesus each also have their moment in the month of December. We assume we know the story, but there's always more. Buried in the Scriptures are hidden treasures waiting to be discovered. These treasures are not the glittering, ephemeral ones—

here today, gone tomorrow. They are the ones that last. Scriptural treasures have the power to kindle the hardest of hearts and awaken the staunchest of cynics. Hebrew scholar Kenneth Bailey reminds us that "what happens to Mary is a foreshadowing, a model of what is to happen to the believing community. They, like her, will be exalted out of their lowliness."[1] Together, let's reclaim hidden treasures with regard to Mary, the mother of Jesus. Our joy depends on it.

VIRGIN BIRTH?

If you were to sum up the story of the holiday season in one word, what word would you use? I am tempted to say *weird*. The virgin-birth claim may be the most unbelievable, atypical, hilarity-inducing aspect of the entire narrative, as virgin pregnancies aren't exactly a common occurrence in human history.

Most people today would agree that Mary's "immaculate conception" is absurd. On this side of the Enlightenment, there is nothing rational about the story. Attempting to explain it as logically reasonable at your neighborhood holiday party might prove futile. However, discounting it altogether, though tempting, is not a helpful option either. If Jesus truly is who the Gospels claim him to be, then the reality of the virgin birth is nonnegotiable, given what Jesus was sent to accomplish—namely, the forgiveness of sin and the renewal of creation.

Many people find aspects of the Christmas story intriguing while also feeling that claims such as the virgin birth are implausible. For example, we like the comforting idea of a

God—if there is a God—who comes to be *with* us (and not against us). But some wonder if we need to believe that Jesus was born of a virgin to appreciate the gospel story. Author Glen Scrivener suggested, "Christians believe in the virgin birth of Jesus. Atheists believe in the virgin birth of the universe. Choose your miracle."[2]

The Incarnation is not about the emergence of yet another great sage or stellar teacher or enlightened mystic. The Gospels tell the story of the eternal, unique Word of God coming to earth in human form. Like all humans, the eternal Word would come by natural birth through the womb of a woman. But unlike us, the eternal Word would come by supernatural conception through the Holy Spirit, planted within the womb of Mary.

By the end of this chapter, I am going to show you why believing the virgin birth influences who we are in Christ today.

ABSURD WONDER

Christmas is not a story of the birth of a spiritual guru who came to spread new and special knowledge for journeys toward self-actualization. It's so much bigger. And it's so much better too. Christmas is the story of the One who has come to liberate creation from the bondage of sin and death, calling all who will hear this good news to open their hearts and receive their new identity by grace. We then are empowered to join God in working for the cause of justice and truth. Gurus can't do that; saviors can.

And as weird as the claim of the virgin birth may sound

to our post-Enlightenment ears, let's not forget that much of what society believes to be self-evident is also absurd (yet true):

Quarks—astonishing
Earth's precise conditions for life—incredible
Gravity—weird
Dark matter—bewildering
Light as both waves and particles—baffling
Quantum entanglement—bizarre

If science (and television) purports these weird mysteries in our universe (or multiverse, or whatever verse we are in by the time you read this book) as realities, we also should consider the greatest mystery of all: an angel long ago hovering over a poor young woman in a forgettable town, pronouncing God's love for the world. This love is then evidenced by a divine seed planted within Mary's womb.

Consider the scriptural connections between the Spirit who hovered over and then descended into creation from the opening lines of Genesis, and the Spirit who hovered over and then descended into Mary in the opening lines of Matthew. It's as if God was restarting creation once again through Mary. These connections, or linkages, from one book of the Bible to another are called *keshers* in Hebrew. The Bible is full of *keshers* because God wrote a unified story, stretching from Genesis to Revelation.

Ben Myers, Australian theologian and scholar, put it this way:

At the beginning of Luke's Gospel, the angel visits Mary and tells her that "the Holy Spirit will come upon you, and the power of the Most High will overshadow you" (Luke 1:35). This opening act of Jesus's story is meant to remind us of another beginning: "In the beginning God created the heavens and the earth. Now the earth was formless and empty, darkness was over the surface of the deep, and the Spirit of God was hovering over the waters" (Gen. 1:1–2). . . .

So when the Spirit broods over the womb of Mary, we see a picture of God's creative work happening all over again. Jesus is brought into being by the creative breath of God's Spirit.[3]

So, you see, the virgin birth is critical to the Christmas story. I'll admit, embracing the absurd is difficult, but who really wants to live in a world without the absurdity of gravity? The virgin birth is one of the most incredible mysteries we can ever embrace. Theologian Stanley Hauerwas was right: "Without Mary's virginity the story cannot be told."[4]

What exactly *is* the story? With all the stress and clutter of the season, we lose sight of the essence. There are aspects to the story that remain unknown that are crucial to reclaim.

CHRISTMAS IS BETTER THAN YOU THINK

The word *annunciation* is sometimes used around Christmastime. Annunciation is a fancy way to say "announcement." The angel's announcement is the miracle that God has planted the earth's savior in Mary's womb. Absurd!

The angel answered, "The Holy Spirit will come on you, and the power of the Most High will overshadow you. So the holy one to be born will be called the Son of God." (Luke 1:35)

Consider Mary's role in this conversation. She receives grace from God in the form of spiritual pregnancy. She was chosen to carry the Christ child in her womb. She, therefore, is a picture of how the gospel of Jesus Christ works. Mary did not *achieve* anything; she *received* everything. The reason Gabriel called her Mary "full of grace" was that God's extravagant grace literally filled her womb (Luke 1:28, DRV).

Mary lived in a region of Galilee saturated with Jews devoted to Torah. It was standard practice for Jewish children as young as five to begin memorizing the books of Moses (that is, the Torah) in the home.[5] Small Jewish communities were filled with children who had the Torah memorized and put it into practice as they anticipated the Messiah's coming.

Science today claims that the average human possesses more than eighty-six billion neurons in the brain.[6] These neurons constantly make connections to navigate life meaningfully. I imagine that for a first-century Galilean, Luke's gospel would bridge some connections between Gabriel's announcement to Mary and other scriptures from the writings of Moses. Again, the Bible is full of *keshers* (connections between one text and another).

To enhance the true meaning of Christmas, consider these three prophetic connections between the Old Testament and Luke's gospel:

CONNECTION 1	
Old Testament Scripture	Luke Scripture
The Spirit of God was hovering over the waters. (Genesis 1:2)	The Holy Spirit will **come on you,** and the power of the Most High will **overshadow** you. (Luke 1:35)

Relevance: In Genesis, the Spirit hovered over creation. In Luke, the Spirit hovered over Mary. Genesis tells of the beginning of creation. Luke tells of the beginning of new creation. Genesis 1 and Luke 1 are connected.

CONNECTION 2	
Old Testament Scripture	Luke Scripture
[The serpent] **said** to the woman, "Did God really say, 'You must not eat from any tree in the garden'?" (Genesis 3:1)	The angel went to her and **said,** "Greetings, you who are highly favored! The Lord is with you." (Luke 1:28)

Relevance: In both verses, angels (the serpent and Gabriel) went to the women (Eve and Mary) and spoke. Remember, Satan is sometimes interpreted as a fallen angel (see Isaiah 14; Ezekiel 28). In Genesis, a rebellious angel (the serpent) whispered deception into Eve's ear and sowed temptation into her heart. In Luke, an obedient angel whispered the reversal into Mary's ear. Gabriel's message was not deception but redemption. Reversing the sowing of temptation in Genesis, in Luke, the Spirit sowed salvation in Mary. The name *Jesus,* therefore, literally means "the Lord is salvation." In Luke, the angel Gabriel announced the reversal of the Fall from Genesis. Just as Jesus was later seen as God's reversal of Adam (see 1 Corinthians 15:45), so Mary became God's reversal of Eve. Genesis 3 and Luke 1 are connected.

CONNECTION 3	
Old Testament Scripture	Luke Scripture
Make the cherubim of one piece with the cover, at the two ends. The cherubim are to have their wings spread upward, **overshadowing** the cover with them. (Exodus 25:19–20)	The Holy Spirit will come on you, and the power of the Most High will **overshadow** you. (Luke 1:35)

Relevance: The ark of the covenant and the body of Mary were both overshadowed by God's presence. In Exodus, the Word of God came in the form of *stone* and was placed in the ark. In Luke, the Word of God came in the form of *flesh* and was placed in the womb. Mary, then, was the new ark of the covenant. Her body became the place where God's presence most fully dwelled. For nine months, she would house the Word. But consider the shift from the old covenant to the new: The Word transitioned from stone and took on flesh (see Ezekiel 36:26). Therefore, Mary was both the reversal of Eve and the fulfillment of the ark.

So far, I have attempted to make three connections between the Old and New Testaments. I have one final connection between Luke's gospel and the book of Acts for you to ponder. First, consider this question: If Mary is the fulfillment of the ark, who, then, might be the fulfillment of Mary?

CONNECTION 4	
Acts Scripture	Luke Scripture
You will receive power when the Holy Spirit **comes on you.** (Acts 1:8)	The Holy Spirit will **come on you,** and the power of the Most High will overshadow you. (Luke 1:35)

Relevance: Like leaving breadcrumbs to guide the reader, Luke intended we notice that what happened to Mary was still happening in a similar but different way for those who also made space to receive good news. Philosopher Dallas Willard observed, "The obviously well kept secret of the 'ordinary' is that it is made to be a receptacle of the divine, a place where the life of God flows."[7] Whoa! That's something to think about.

SO WHAT?

Let's put these connections together:

- The ark of the covenant carried the Word of God in *stone* (see Exodus 25:10–22).
- The womb of Mary carried the Word of God in *flesh* (see Luke 1:26–38).
- The Messiah's people carry the Word of God in *Spirit* (see Acts 1:1–11).

The apostle Paul picked up the thread and posed this staggering question: "Do you not know that you are God's temple and that *God's Spirit dwells in you*?" (1 Corinthians 3:16, ESV). To the church in Colossae, Paul wrote, "God has chosen to make known . . . the glorious riches of this mystery, *which is Christ in you,* the hope of glory" (Colossians 1:27). Just as Mary—full of grace—carried God the Son around in her body, so we—full of grace—carry God the Spirit around in ours.

Perhaps, like Mary, you're asking, "How can this be?" Gabriel's answer to Mary is the same for us today. Say yes to God and receive the Holy Spirit. You cannot achieve entrance to God's kingdom. It's all grace. No, we do not perform our way into God's kingdom. God freely offers the Holy Spirit to indwell all who call upon the name of Jesus, the Son. May you follow Mary's lead and respond likewise: "I am the Lord's servant. . . . May your word to me be fulfilled" (Luke 1:38).

ARKS AND PRAYER CLOSETS

Jesus taught that we possess a prayer closet within us. Specifically, he said that when we pray, we should go into our room and close the door to do it (see Matthew 6:6). I think he also meant that in addition to finding a secret place to pray, we should pray from the deepest part of our being. In this season, we are busy and tempted to pray shallow prayers on the way out the door. We are tempted to stress and worry, so we pray quickly without taking time to get in touch with core longings.

In modern Hebrew, the word for "ark" is *aron.* In Jewish synagogues, the *aron* is a place where the scrolls of the Bible are kept. It can also mean "closet." When Jesus invites us to pray in our closet, is he telling us to go to the synagogue (or church) closet and pray inside it? No. Again, he is remind-ing us that we are "made to be a receptacle of the divine."[8]

The Holy Spirit indwells us. Therefore, redeemed hu-manity is now the ark of the new covenant. You are where God most dwells. Christmas is only the beginning. The God who came to be *with us* is the same God who dwells *in us*.

If all this is true, wouldn't it be tragic to spend this season amid the noise? Perhaps the greatest invitation during Advent is to slow down, daily find a quiet place, and attend to the depths within your being; and, like Mary, treasure the mystery of God's indwelling presence in your heart. As you do, also like Mary, wherever you go, you will find yourself spiritually giving birth to God's presence in the form of fruit such as "love, joy, peace, patience, kindness, goodness, faithfulness, gentleness, [and] self-control" (Gala-tians 5:22–23, ESV).

Reflection

Spend some time reading Luke 1:26–38, and then reflect on the sketch below. All sacred doing starts with sacred being. When we take time to be with God, we rediscover the mystery of Christ living in us as at the center of our being. How might stillness in this season prepare you to praise God for the mighty wonders around you?

2

JOSEPH: CHARACTER

The Practice of Relational Intentionality
Matthew 1:18–25

IT WAS EXHAUSTING. ELAINA AND I WELCOMED OUR daughter, Eloise, into the world in a crowded hospital in New York City. My wife's labor was a thirty-six-hour marathon, ending in a vacuum birth. After spending a couple more days in a shared hospital room—yes, shared—we brought home a beautiful baby girl to an apartment the size of a college dormitory.

The months that followed are now a blur. Eloise would choke on spittle in her sleep, so, being first-time parents, we thought it wise to rotate three-hour shifts through the night. In an eight-week span, I watched all seven seasons of *The West Wing*. During the day, however, I was half human, half zombie. My ratio might be off here. No matter—it wasn't pretty. For those two months, I was the grumpiest husband, father, and pastor the world has ever known. I do recall some banter Elaina and I shared in the middle of those months as to whether our marriage would survive sleep deprivation.

Parenting is hard.

Many say it brings out the best in us. Maybe. But it first reveals the worst in us. Parenting shows us the kind of people we want to be but are still in the process of becoming. Here are some examples:

I'm not always kind, but I want to be.
I'm not always patient, but I want to be.
I'm not always gentle, but I want to be.

Becoming a dad felt like holding a mirror to my face and staring at the truth that my spiritual formation had a (very) long way to go. For me, being a dad is like rebuilding a plane in the air: It seems impossible. Accepting the call to parent is the most challenging thing I've ever undertaken. I don't mean that children are challenging (though they can be). Parenting is challenging because it exposes our self-serving tendencies cultivated over decades. Through the crucible of humility (and humiliation), parenting requires us to confront and develop character slowly over time. I thought I was a decent guy, but then I had a baby. Turns out I'm an impatient jerk. Anyone else?

"This is not a parenting book," you might say. "Get back to the Christmas story." Well, at the center of the Christmas story is the birth of a child and, by consequence, the "birth" of new parents. The call to parenthood (and cultivating relationships) is of central importance to the story. Matthew guides us brilliantly:

> This is how the birth of Jesus the Messiah came about: His mother Mary was pledged to be married to Joseph, but before they came together, she was found to be pregnant through the Holy Spirit. (Matthew 1:18)

BUT

Every good story has an arc. The most basic arc is exposition, climax, resolution. As a story unfolds toward the climax, a reader is typically confronted by a conflict demanding resolution. In Jesus's birth story in Matthew, the conflict is obvious: "Mary was pledged to be married to Joseph, but . . ." This was no small "but." Mary was pregnant through a means other than her husband. In the first-century Galilean world of the Jews, this situation was grounds for divorce at minimum and death at maximum.

The "buts" of life are the crossroads of formation. It is in the challenging places, both expected and unexpected, where our character is revealed and can grow. In Matthew 1, Joseph found himself at a crossroads. We are privileged to witness his journey to eventually accept the profound invitation to become the stepfather of the Son of God. And although this became a source of tremendous blessing, it probably came at great cost:

> Because Joseph her husband was faithful to the law, and yet did not want to expose her to public disgrace, he had in mind to divorce her quietly. But after he had considered this, an angel of the Lord appeared to him in a dream and said, "Joseph son of David, do not be afraid to take Mary home as your wife, because what is conceived in her is from the Holy Spirit." (Matthew 1:19–20)

JOSEPH THE HUSBAND

To be sure, we know very little about Joseph's life. But from a few scriptures and the context of Galilee in the first century, we can stitch together some possibilities about the kind of man Joseph must have been and why God chose him for the sacred task. As Joseph neared fatherhood, there was a maturity to him that I did not possess at his age. The first was his lack of vengeance after learning that Mary (technically, his wife) was pregnant (technically, not by him)—which is enough to make a male's blood boil.

Joseph was an upstanding, law-abiding Jewish male. The first place he looked for guidance after learning about this scandal was the law, which says,

> If there is a betrothed virgin, and a man meets her in the city and lies with her [agreement], then you shall bring them both out to the gate of that city, and you shall stone them to death with stones. . . . So you shall purge the evil from your midst. (Deuteronomy 22:23–24, esv)

Whereas Joseph was a man of the Scriptures, his interpretation of the text was to hold it with mercy (see Micah 6:8). So he decided to "divorce her quietly" (Matthew 1:19). Notice he did this for Mary's sake and not his own. He did not want her to face public shame during her pregnancy. Joseph's motive was to spare her of shame rather than minimize his own. He hoped that perhaps he and Mary could go their separate ways without too much controversy.

At this point, it may be helpful to grasp some insights into first-century Jewish marriage.

MARRIAGE

The marriage between Jews in the first century was a two-fold process. The first part of the process was the betrothal (kiddushin). Difficult as it may be to imagine, marriages were often arranged by the fathers of the groom and bride. Ancient Near East cultures were not individualist cultures, seeking foremost the advancement of one's own desires. Rather, they were collectivist cultures, seeking foremost the advancement of the group identity.[1] In the case of marriage, this meant the entire family. Therefore, the groom and his father would visit the bride and her father to ask for the marriage. If the father of the bride agreed—often (and thankfully) with the approval of the bride—a matchmaker (*shadkan*) would write the marriage contract (ketubah), specifying the terms of the marriage, such as the dowry (mohar).

The dowry was offered by the groom's family to compensate for the financial loss of the bride's domestic output. This period of betrothal would last about a year's time. During that time, the groom would return to his father's house and "prepare a place" for them. Do you hear the echo here to what Jesus would later say to his disciples (John 14:3)? Should the dowry price be agreeable, a cup of wine was poured and the future groom and bride would drink from it.

The groom would drink first, then the bride. According to scholar John DeLancey, "If she accepted the terms and after purifying themselves separately in the ritual bath (*miqveh*), a brief public ceremony followed. Under a canopy (*chuppah*), their pledge to one another was made public. They were now officially betrothed!"[2] However, during the betrothal (equivalent to today's marriage status), it is crucial to note that the couple did not engage in sexual relations. Betrothal entailed commitment without consummation. Intercourse would happen later, then binding together physically what had already taken place spiritually during the betrothal. That is how we know Jesus was not biologically fathered by Joseph. That is also why Joseph would initially be dumbfounded when discovering that Mary was pregnant.

In the year of betrothal, should the bride engage in sexual

activity with another man, the groom was entitled to a refund of the dowry, and he could also take her to the court of the Jews for sentencing. That is specifically what Joseph chose *not* to do. His humiliation must have been great, but his humility was greater. Joseph was a deeply formed man after God's own heart. No wonder he was a descendant of David.

DO NOT BE AFRAID

An angel appeared to Joseph in a dream and told him not to be afraid. What would Joseph be afraid of? Well, people, of course—namely, religious people. Socially speaking, he was about to enter a firestorm of gossip, slander, and judgment in the court of public opinion. The decision Joseph made to remain in the marriage was far more controversial than we can understand distanced by place and time.

Joseph was a man of humility and integrity. When he learned that Mary had not been unfaithful and that she carried in her womb the Savior of the world (see Matthew 1:21– 23), he "woke up [and] did what the angel of the Lord had commanded him and took Mary home as his wife" (verse 24). That is what a father does. True fathers are humble and loyal.

So, why does any of this matter in regard to the Christmas story?

We live in a world of shallow commitment, fluid loyalty, and inflated self-interest. In society today, men increasingly struggle to show up holistically in marriage and parenting. In these few passages that include Joseph, we learn that he was a man of deep humility, fierce loyalty, and self-sacrifice. Truly, his call in the story was as necessary as Mary's. Joseph wasn't perfect. But my hunch is that God (whom Jesus called "Father") found in Joseph a man who would become an earthly father who provided glimpses of what our heavenly Father is like.

JOSEPH THE FATHER

We all go through times of feeling spiritually dry. And rather than passively complaining about it when I feel this way, I've learned to proactively seek refreshing. When I sense dryness in my soul, I try to change things up. Sometimes it's a shift in my routine. Other times it's a change of scenery, or a day in solitude at a monastery. But on rare occasions, I feel so dry that I buy a cheap flight somewhere and tell God I'm going to find him there for the day. Is that weird? I think maybe it is.

One day I came across an article about a light show at a cathedral in Montreal, Canada. Yes, I said light show. Suspend your judgment and hear me out. Maybe I was intrigued by the odd combination of lights and cathedral. I learned that thousands of people were lining up to experience the luminous spectacle set to orchestral music. Crazy as it may sound, I booked a flight and weeks later attended the event with a friend.

I was unsure what precisely I was searching for; I just knew I needed a fresh jolt of the heart that I couldn't get through reading another book or sitting quietly by a pond. I was hopeful, but my expectations were vague. The cathedral doors opened and, a thousand strong, we snaked our way through an endless queue until we finally entered the sacred space. For the first twenty minutes, we meandered around the interior walls of the church, gazing at the hanging art. And just before we took our seats, it happened . . . BAM! In the same way a spiritual defibrillator revives a heart, my dry soul awakened to life as my eyes transfixed upon the strangest of paintings.

In his arms, Joseph held the infant Jesus. That was it. The dryness of my soul was watered in one image. Joseph held Jesus. I'd never really thought about it. I guess I always imagined Joseph as a passive stepdad: present in the story but located at a distance from Mary and Jesus in any given scene. I know not all stepdads are passive or distant, but in my mind, Joseph rarely made it into the family photo. Sure, he was faithful, but only Mary was central, right? The painting was undoing all of that for me. My artist friend Rick, the guy who drew the doodles for this book, recently said to me that he imagined Joseph's situation to be like the effect of a Russian nesting doll, where Joseph held Mary, and Mary held Jesus. But did Joseph also hold Jesus? It's a great question.

Thus far, we've established that Joseph was humble and loyal. But could he have been affectionate also? If the painting is accurate, then yes, he was! And seeing it was worth the price of admission. In the blink of an eye, the father heart of Joseph was restoring for me the Father heart of God. God had been calling me to become humble and loyal for my family, but he was also reminding me that his posture toward me is no different. In fact, God is the perfect parent. As Father, he holds creation, embracing each one of us intimately. He is not indifferent, passive, or distant. God the Father sent the Son as the climax to the story's arc that he is active, present, and willing to embrace us no matter the cost.

In the biographical movie *Father Stu,* the lead character, played by Mark Wahlberg, waxes poetic, "Imagine how it must have felt for Joseph . . . to be the less important father."[3] Again, I'd never really thought about it. Humble, loyal, and affectionate, Joseph was a remarkable example of spiritual maturity. Perhaps his presence deserves more attention in the Advent season.

Reflection

Spend some time reading Matthew 1:18–25, and then reflect on the sketch below. Ask yourself, How is God asking me to soften my heart toward a challenging situation or person? What gift might await me if I were to step toward peace?

3

INNKEEPER: HOSPITALITY

The Practice of Radical Welcome

Luke 2:7

IN NOVEMBER 2003, A CHRISTMAS ROMANTIC COM-edy released that has been rerunning around the holiday season ever since. *Love Actually,* although a classic for many, is also a conflicting film. A combination of hilarity, irony, and vulgarity, the film includes one scene that is particularly disturbing to me, but it's not the scene you might think. The scene that disturbs me most occurs late in the film, at the local-public-school Christmas pageant.

Assembled onstage are the usual Christmas suspects: Mary, Joseph, shepherds, some sheep, and a plastic baby Jesus swaddled snug in a manger. But then, randomly, next to the familiar cast is a strange mash-up of characters, ranging from orange lobsters to a green squid, from a creepy-looking whale to a kid in Spider-Man face paint, wearing a crown. The scene is rather absurd, leaving the audience to wonder why these sea creatures were present at the birth of Christ. After all, Bethlehem is not located on the Mediterranean Sea. The film writers added these extra characters to the scene. Funny, but disturbing.

I mention these extra characters not to be critical but because the film reminds me of an extra character who has, for generations, been inserted into the biblical story: the innkeeper. And that disturbs me because—spoiler alert—the innkeeper didn't exist. At least, not in the way we think according to our Christmas pageants in the West. This claim may surprise you, ruining the memory of your childhood nostalgia. But nowhere in the Bible do we find a keeper of an inn refusing hospitality to Mary and Joseph. Instead, Scripture tells of a homeowner in Bethlehem who was out of space but welcomed the couple into his home anyway.

The story is not a tale of a curmudgeon motel operator refusing room to a pregnant couple. It's just the opposite. How, then, you might wonder, did we get this so wrong, and for so long? Let's look at the text:

> She wrapped him in cloths and placed him in a manger, because there was no guest room available for them. (Luke 2:7)

Did you catch that? The entire scene hinges on the words "no guest room." Out of that phrase, we invented an innkeeper who ran a motel with no vacancy and who pointed the couple down the road to birth the child in a random barn. But is that how it happened?

One option for interpretation, which I do not share, is that this man was a family member of Joseph who did not want to associate himself with a baby conceived before *chuppah,* in this case meaning the wedding ceremony. So, perhaps they did find a cave (not a barn) in which to birth the Christ child. Maybe that's how it all went down. But I don't think that's quite right. There is another option.

LET'S GET TECHNICAL

The Greek word used here for "guest room" is *kataluma.* Later in Luke, in the parable of the good Samaritan (see 10:25–37), we do find a Greek word used for "inn." It is the word *pandocheion.* So, if Luke wanted us to imagine an actual innkeeper who had no rooms available, he would have used the word *pandocheion.* But he didn't. He used a different word. He used *kataluma,* which means guest room (not inn)!

Luke did not intend for us to think that a motel manager at the La Quinta was turning away the holy family. Instead, the host of the home was likely a family member of Joseph who simply had no extra room in his house to offer because it was most likely already taken by another respected family member, probably elderly, who had arrived before them. Remember, Quirinius of Syria had ordered a census of the land. Jews everywhere were returning to their villages of family origin. Therefore, it is very possible that Bethlehem was swelling with extra people and that guest rooms in homes were limited.

To understand the text, consider the sketch below of a first-century Middle Eastern dwelling common in the Judea region. The couple requested to stay in the guest room (*kataluma*), but it was already occupied. Luke then tells us that after the birth, Mary placed Jesus in the manger (animal trough). The implication here is that Jesus, the King of kings, the Lord of lords, the Maker of heaven and earth, was born in the animal room.

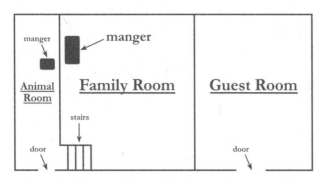

David Croteau, *Urban Legends of the New Testament: 40 Common Misconceptions* (Nashville: B&H Publishing, 2015), 7.

Dwellings were often built on uneven slopes of limestone. Upon entering a house, an individual would walk a few steps up to the family room. In this main room, a family would eat, sleep, and cook. Comically speaking, the "open floor plan" is not something new; it was alive and well in the first century. As illustrated above, families could then add on a guest room that would be next to the family room or built on top of the roof.[1]

Notice what took place on the ground floor: That area was where animals could stay. Before the days of central heating, the body heat of animals could provide warmth like a furnace to the home in the cold months. At the close of the day, a beast or two would be invited into the home for the night. A manger would be present in the home to feed the livestock. Once dawn broke, the animals would burst out of the home for the day.

Now maybe you're thinking, *This is just nonsense, AJ. It cannot be true. It defies everything I've been taught. Can we prove this anywhere else in the Scriptures?*

Yes, as it turns out, we can.

BURSTING BEASTS

In Judges 11, we meet a guy named Jephthah, who was at the epicenter of an obscure and controversial story. He vowed to God that if the Ammonites were delivered into his hands, he would sacrifice, upon his return home, the first thing that burst out of the door. As irony would have it, that "thing" turned out to be his daughter. So excited to see him, she burst forth, out the door before the beasts, in order to embrace her father's victorious return!

So, why would he have offered to sacrifice the first thing

out his door? Because he didn't expect that it would be his daughter! *Why not?* you might wonder. Because animals (not humans) seeking pasture were the first to burst out the door in the morning.

My wife and daughter love dogs. They are partial to the Yorkshire terrier. I like to act ambivalent to pets, but I'm not. When our first Yorkie died, I wept for weeks. And I'm serious. I had no idea how deeply these little creatures can nestle in our souls without our knowing it. Our latest Yorkie is named Magnolia. She weighs in at three pounds (on a good day). When the doorbell rings, Maggie is the first to the door. Unless I take my foot and shove her to the side, she always beats me, bursting through as it opens. Now, imagine trying to win against a cow or sheep. Unlikely. That tells us just how excited Jephthah's daughter must have been to see her father: so excited that she probably pushed the animals out of the way and burst through the animal room. Whoops!

Radical Welcome

Thus far, I have established that the host was not an operator of an inn (*pandocheion*), refusing a room to the couple. Rather, because the census was drawing people like Joseph home, the host (most likely a family member and not a random stranger) did not have a guest room (*kataluma*) available. Therefore, the couple slept near the animal section of the house and eventually gave birth there.

This leads to yet another observation. The village of Bethlehem would have been small, numbering only several hundred in population. Because they were just five miles from Jerusalem, the villagers observed strict religious laws, including those pertaining to pregnant women. Mary and Joseph were technically married (betrothed) but not yet at the stage where intercourse was practiced. The villagers would have known that the couple had yet to undergo the ceremony (*chuppah*). Therefore, Mary would have been considered not only unclean but also deserving to be stoned, according to the law.

That makes the hospitality of the host much more controversial. He was harboring an unlawful couple. We can only wonder what the villagers thought. Was the host the victim of gossip or synagogue expulsion or even physical threats? We don't know, but it is possible. On top of that, consider the fact that the Son of God was born alongside the stench of wild livestock. The whole scenario is nearly beyond belief.

Radical welcome often comes at a price. Jesus welcomed sinners and was criticized. He healed on the Sabbath and was threatened. He ate in the homes of sinners and was slandered. Jesus sat with an adulterous woman near a well in Samaria and was accosted by his closest friends. So yes, radical welcome is costly. This is true even today, but it's the way of the kingdom.

The greatest evangelistic strategy of the early church was not the community's ability to transmit theological *convictions,* truthful as they were. Rather, it was the community's willingness to embody *compassion*. Hospitality changes the world. Radical welcome, not violence, eventually brought the Roman world to its knees before King Jesus. That is how the kingdom works.

Jesus said the world would come to know God through the way we love one another (see John 13:35). Love really is the greatest evangelistic strategy on earth. In the second century A.D., Tertullian, perhaps the greatest apologist the world has ever known, imagined pagans watching the lives of Christians and uttering, "See how they love one another!"[2] Love doesn't mean we renounce conviction, but it does mean we embody compassion. In an increasingly polarized world, many people are deceived to think that conviction and compassion cannot coexist. For example, some errantly believe that the greater our conviction, the lesser our compassion; and the greater our compassion, the lesser our conviction. But that is a lie. Jesus is the model. He was a man of paramount conviction but at the same time held more compassion than any person who ever lived. Great conviction necessitates even greater levels of compassion.

The host of the house without any room represented the heart of Jesus. It's so fitting that Jesus, the most hospitable one, was born under the roof of a man of radical hospitality. Decades after Jesus's resurrection, the writer of Hebrews encourages us to "not forget to show hospitality to strangers, for by so doing some people have shown hospitality to angels without knowing it" (13:2). The practice of welcome changes the world. The early church rescued discarded babies (usually girls) from trash heaps. The early church cared for the poor before cities provided welfare. The early church cared for the elderly before the days of social security. The early church fed and clothed prisoners before the tax-funded state penitentiary. A time is coming when the church must again rise and care for the least of these. As it declines in number in the West, now is the time.

The expansion of the church will not be through well-crafted theological argumentation; no, it will come through compassion. It will look like intentional invitations to meal sharing with grace. It will look like orphan care and relationship beyond the church's mailing address. It will look like attention given to the least of these and leaning in curiously with our political opposite. It will probably look like more questions than statements. Jesus will be the center. Our convictions and positions matter, but so does our compassion and posture. Truly, how we hold our positions is as important as the positions we hold.

Jesus gets this. The early church got this. The "innkeeper," who didn't exist, got this. This man who owned a crowded house was a gracious host to a Jewish family in need. He could have taken the law seriously and refused them room, but he didn't. In welcoming the couple into his home, he wasn't reducing or minimizing the law; he was obeying it. This man chose to follow the law deeply and love his neighbor as himself (see Leviticus 19:18). And his neighbors from Galilee needed a warm place to birth the Son of God. Of course, he didn't know the full extent at the time, but he does now. The "angel" he welcomed into his home that day turned out to be God's Son. Radical welcome changes the world. It always has. It always will. This is love, actually.

Reflection

Meditate on Luke 2:7, and then reflect on the sketch below. Who might God be inviting you to radically welcome this season?

4

ZECHARIAH: SILENCE

The Practice of Stilling the Mind
Luke 1:5–25

I DEEPLY ADMIRE SCHOOLTEACHERS, BUT I DON'T envy them. Capturing the fleeting attention of a fourth grader like me must've been daunting for a teacher. I recall countless times of being penalized during recess with a time-out because I couldn't control side talking, disrupting, or laughing during class time. The consequence for these behaviors was silence and solitude while everyone else got to run, laugh, and play. Whereas I fully deserved time-outs, the subconscious message I received as a child was that silence and solitude were never rewards but instead strictly penalties for bad behavior.

Reflecting on my youth, I think my contemplative journey began in the fifth grade. Mrs. Schott was a legendary teacher. Patient, wise, and nurturing, she was aware of the chemicals raging in the brains of ten-year-olds. But rather than penalizing students with a time-out when we couldn't focus, she instead played classical music on cassette tapes. (Remember those?) In the blink of an eye, the classroom atmosphere would transition from a loud ruckus to a quiet hush. And all she did was press Play. It was incredible. Bach's Concerto for Two Violins stabilized the young masses with sounds of bliss encouraging our little brains to focus on the task of long division.

It was the first time that befriending silence felt like a gift, not a penalty. I was learning to channel my attention and embrace the gift of quiet, of contemplation, which is the gift of stilling the mind and embracing the silence. That is the gift that the story of Zechariah from Luke's gospel has to offer us:

Both of them [Zechariah and Elizabeth] were righteous in the sight of God, observing all the Lord's commands and decrees blamelessly. But they were childless because Elizabeth was not able to conceive, and they were both very old. (1:6–7)

BARRENNESS AND BITTERNESS

Zechariah, who descended from the long priestly line of Aaron, lived within one day's walk from Jerusalem, most likely in a mountain village called Ein Karem.[1] But unlike many of his priestly colleagues, Zechariah was not upper-class. I'll spare you the Hasmonean dynasty history lesson here, but let me sum it up by stating how thoroughly corrupt the priestly system had become at the time of Jesus's birth. Many priests, seeking wealth and power instead of justice and holiness, sought to harmonize Greco-Roman culture (that is, Hellenism) with their Hebrew way of life.[2] Hard to do, but try they did. The priests who sought to do that were commonly referred to as Sadducees. The Scriptures are clear, however, that Zechariah and his wife, Elizabeth, were not like many of the Sadducees who syncretized cultures, played party politics, and gained great wealth. The couple did not follow the corrupted path. Instead, they were "righteous" and "blameless" before God, according to Luke 1:6.

So, if Zechariah and Elizabeth were blameless, why were they barren? That is the question Scripture invites us to ponder. Barrenness was perceived as a sign of God's displeasure. The whispering gossip in the village must have been deafening for them. The neighbors surely wondered whether this couple hid secret darkness that had yet to come to light. Did their barrenness cause others to question Zechariah's integrity for performing the priestly duties? Questions like these can torment the soul.

I imagine that the anxiety took a toll on Zechariah's well-being as he and Elizabeth slowly aged without the blessing of children. Like them, we carry so many things around in our bodies that no one knows about. And the negative self-talk can crush our spirits:

What is wrong with me?
Where are you, God?
Why am I depressed?
When will life improve?
How did I get here?
Why does it have to be this way?

With Zechariah void of Bach concerto cassettes to quiet his soul, his barrenness must have devolved into bitterness. I don't know, but I wonder. Perhaps the old man the angel visited that day was a shriveled version of a once vibrant, hopeful priest:

Once when Zechariah's division was on duty and he was serving as priest before God, he was chosen by lot, according to the custom of the priesthood, to go into the temple of the Lord and burn incense. And when the time for the burning of incense came, all the assembled worshipers were praying outside. (verses 8–10)

ZECHARIAH THE PRIEST

In the first century, the number of priests was estimated to be upward of twenty thousand. They were grouped into twenty-four divisions that rotated weekly to serve the temple. Each division served temple duty twice per year for one week's time. While serving, the priests would sleep there.[3] Think of it as temple camp for adults.

When the time came for the division of Abijah to serve, the straw that Zechariah drew was the prestigious role of burning incense in the room before the Holy of Holies. This was no small deal. It was the honor of a lifetime that might never happen to him again. He would spend the week next to the holiest place on earth, lighting candles and offering prayers up to God for the people twice per day.

Have you ever felt as though your prayers go nowhere? Burning incense is a symbol of prayer to rebuke that lie. Imagine watching the smoke ascend heavenward as you prayed. The ritual was invented to remind us that our prayers go somewhere.

But the irony here is thick. Think about it: Zechariah carried the stigma of barrenness, yet he was the one chosen to perform a most sacred and sought-after priestly duty. His prayers to God for a child over decades had returned void, yet he was called upon to steward the prayers of God's people to God in the temple—in the room next to the holiest place on earth. The inadequacy he felt to perform the task must have been unsettling. The text sets up a dynamic tension in Zechariah that we are meant to notice.

THE PRESENCE OF GOD

Before the Holy Spirit descended on the Day of Pentecost around A.D. 33, the presence of God dwelled most densely in the Jerusalem temple. Within the temple was a room called the Holy of Holies. This room, housing the ark of the covenant, was believed to be the most sacred place. The closer one got to this room, the closer one got to God's presence. Think of God's presence as zones of proximity (see the image on the following page). It is not that God's presence was confined to only one place on earth but that it was more concentrated in the Holy of Holies than anywhere else. In fact, he was so present in that room that only one designated man once a year was able to enter it and live. In Luke's gospel, Zechariah was called upon to spend the week in a room called the Holy Place, which was directly next to the Holy of Holies. The concentric circles below help us understand how the Jews thought about proximity to God's presence around the time Jesus was born. Again, the closer one got to the room called the Holy of Holies, the closer one was to God's presence.

These are the zones of proximity to God.

10 the earth

9 the land of Israel

8 the city of Jerusalem

7 the Temple Mount (a wall called Sorek that warned Gentiles to step no further)

6 the Court of the Women

5 the Court of the Israelites (Jewish men only)

4 the Court of the Priests (where Zechariah would be granted entrance as a priest)

3 the area between the porch and the altar

2   the sanctuary / Holy Place (where Zechariah would
    enter to burn incense)

1   the Holy of Holies

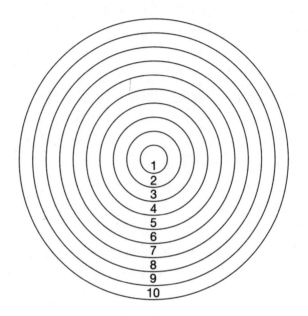

Again, prior to Pentecost, God's presence dwelled more densely in one location than in all the others. For Zechariah to spend an entire week next door to the place God most dwelled must have been incredible (and perhaps frightening). Luke's gospel then states,

An angel of the Lord appeared to him, standing at the right side of the altar of incense. When Zechariah saw him, he was startled and was gripped with fear. (1:11–12)

Why was he startled? I get that an angel's appearance might be startling. But if Zechariah was in the room next to the Holy of Holies—closer than he had ever been to God's presence—why would it be surprising to see an angel there? Isn't that the very place on earth one might expect to encounter one?

Think about all the disappointment, shame, and confusion Zechariah carried into the Holy Place. He had been faithful to the priesthood for decades but still bore the painful scars of barrenness. I wonder if Zechariah was startled by the angel because he no longer expected God's presence to show up in his life! Ever been there? I have.

And why didn't Zechariah expect God's presence? Because maybe he was disappointed, weary, and bitter. Maybe Zechariah, priest though he was, was also a human being. Perhaps he was more like us than we think, especially when we feel as though God hears other people's prayers but not our own. At that place in our spiritual lives, a spiritual equation goes like this:

Years of Religious Service +
    Life Disappointments =
Bitterness, Cynicism, and Disbelief

It's tempting to judge Zechariah harshly since we see the whole story, but maybe we are meant to see ourselves in him. It's not easy to have hope and joy when we feel as though God has passed us over, especially if we are living "righteous and blameless" lives. *God, I did my part, so why haven't you done yours?* we think.

Maybe that's the place you find yourself at right now. If not, at some point it will be. Disappointment is hard, particularly when we feel we've done all the right things. We've gone to church, prayed the creed, read the Bible, and given of our time and money. Perhaps this is part of what Bono meant when he sang, "I still haven't found what I'm looking for."[4]

"I've been looking for an heir, Lord," Zechariah cried, "but still we are barren." Our sorrows soon lead to blame placing: Sometimes we blame God, sometimes we blame others, but often we blame ourselves. It's a punishing cycle. And the blame game takes its toll. Over time, we become bitter, and then our bitterness leads to busyness. That is how many people endure the Christmas season. *Just stay busy, we* think. Merry and bright? More like heavy and bitter!

Slowly, over the years, what began as a grief can mutate into a gripe. Grieving is biblical, but griping is not. Grief is an expression, but griping is a way of life. We are meant to grieve to avoid gripe. The psalmists gave us permission to grieve and mourn—loudly even. The prophets tore their clothes, Jeremiah penned Lamentations, and even Jesus wept. But when we do not process our grief and mourn well, we suppress our emotion, and it can turn into a griping lifestyle.

Some people gripe their way through life, grunting, grouchy, and grumbling the whole way through. You can bet that people in our lives who live this way have repressed true grief and then the soul slowly dies. A life of griping decreases our capacity for surprise, awe, and wonder. Maybe that is the place where Zechariah found himself. He was a priest, but he was also a human.

Zechariah's story leads to one obvious conclusion: He was startled by the angelic presence because his expectations for God to move departed long before he lit the incense. Perhaps he was just trying to stay busy, going through the religious motions. That kind of thing still happens all the time. But there's hope. Zechariah's story is a redemptive one:

> The angel said to him: "Do not be afraid, Zechariah; your prayer has been heard. Your wife Elizabeth will bear you a son, and you are to call him John. . . . He will bring back many of the people of Israel to the Lord their God. And he will go on before the Lord, in the spirit and power of Elijah, to turn the hearts of the parents to their children and the disobedient to the wisdom of the righteous—to make ready a people prepared for the Lord."
>
> Zechariah asked the angel, "How can I be sure of this? I am an old man and my wife is well along in years."
> (verses 13, 16–18)

Incredible! "Your prayer has been heard" (verse 13). The first move of the angel was to rebuke the lies Zechariah had been telling himself. Despite the circumstances we face, God hears our prayers. Now, this is the point in the story where we become even more critical about Zechariah. Removed by time and space, we assume our response to the angel would be different. Perhaps we would be more receptive or more open. But would we?

Zechariah found Gabriel's announcement hard to believe. After all, he was super old. Had tons of wrinkles. Probably some skin tags. Gray hair for sure, but maybe even balding. So old that even pickleball would be physically challenging. I imagine him leaning in toward the angel for clarity: "So, Gabriel, how exactly is this all going to work?" Here is what the angel said:

> I am Gabriel. I stand in the presence of God, and I have been sent to speak to you and to tell you this good news. And now you will be silent and not able to speak until the day this happens, because you did not believe my words, which will come true at their appointed time. (verses 19–20)

After burning the incense, the priest was expected to exit the Holy Place and pronounce a blessing over those gathered to pray.[5] The silencing of Zechariah would have caused an awkward moment at the temple that day. Imagine a pastor climbing the pulpit to preach and not being able to speak. (Maybe you would rejoice, but it would still be awkward.) Zechariah would have been unable to perform this moment in the liturgy, and people would have returned home talking about it.

But consider this question: Was the silencing of Zechariah a punishment, or was it a gift? Many quickly conclude it was a punishment. For years, I imagined it that way. But now I am not so sure. My fourth-grade self viewed silence strictly as a punishment for bad behavior. But is that what was happening here? Maybe the Bach concerto was ready to play. Maybe years of gripe were about to be silenced so that Zechariah could grieve meaningfully long enough to receive the gift God was about to conceive.

What if the silencing of Zechariah was a gift to improve his hearing and receptivity?

The Scriptures are chock-full of paradoxes, reversals, and ironies: The last shall be first, lose your life to save it, the greatest will serve, the poor are blessed, and the humble will be exalted, to name a few.

The muting of Zechariah is one of the central themes of the Advent season. His story is an invitation for us to find ourselves within it. We are busy, we are wounded, and we are disappointed, yet we are invited to become quiet to open space to receive the gift God gives. Resist the season's demands for stress, spending, and schedule overload.

God is seldom discovered in the noise; rather, he's discovered in the quiet. Maybe the reason many of us feel a shallow disappointment after December 25 is that we fill our lives up to the brim and then sense something missing when it's over.

Notice what happened after nine long months of silence:

When it was time for Elizabeth to have her baby, she gave birth to a son. . . .

Then they made signs to his father, to find out what he would like to name the child. He asked for a writing tablet, and to everyone's astonishment he wrote, "His name is John." Immediately his mouth was opened and his tongue set free, and he began to speak, praising God. . . .

His father Zechariah was filled with the Holy Spirit and prophesied. (verses 57, 62–64, 67)

After a nine-month quarantine of silence, Zechariah burst forth with a mouth filled with prophecy and praise! *How did that happen?* we wonder. Well, the silence opened space in him to become full of God's word to the point of overflow! Jesus later said his living water would pour out of us. Isn't that what we long for? What was previously for Zechariah a dried-out canyon of bitterness, cynicism, and religious obligation was slowly transformed into a river of living water welling up from the depths of his heart and gushing forth from his mouth. Like a spiritual geyser, praise erupted. Like a seed, God's presence lives inside us waiting to expand. Silent prayer and reflective stillness are the soil for nurturing the growth of that divine life within.

GO SLOW TO GROW

When my daughter was very young, we lived in West Michigan. The winds of winter coming off Lake Michigan create conditions optimal for a snowy season. On Christmas Eve, I often found myself up until the wee hours of the night assembling toddler toys. Exhausted from hours with an Allen wrench, I would finally go to bed. But one Christmas morning, I awoke early. Very early. Wide awake, I felt a nudge in my soul calling me downstairs to sit in the silence. In the cold, I prepared the French press, plugged in the tree lights, and sat in the quiet, looking out to a blanket of fresh, white snow.

It was quiet. It was slow. It was sacred.

A spiritual hush came over me. I felt a soul silence expanding my heart to experience God's presence. No longer confined to the walls of the Holy of Holies, the most concentrated place for God's presence is now the human heart, if we will welcome him.

We will not grow much spiritually if we are busy. We will not hear God's voice clearly if we hurry. The primary task of a Christian in Advent is growing one's capacity to perceive the story by slowing down long enough to receive it. Too much talking, doubting, spending, and stressing crowds out Immanuel—God with us!

I no longer believe that God's silencing of Zechariah was a punishment for unbelief. Rethinking the text, I now believe that Zechariah's silence was intended for his good, to increase his capacity to receive the gift of a promised son. Silence invites fullness. Slowing paves the way to growth.

TWO TOWERS

Two menacing towers can hover high in the season of Christmas. The first is bitterness. Despite Zechariah's spending a lifetime of faithfully attending to religious duties, his wife remained barren, undoubtedly leading to years of social shame, community gossip, and unanswered prayers—surely a recipe for bitterness. The second is busyness. Busyness can be a subconscious strategy to avoid reality. Slowing down opens space for contemplation and reflection. But when we are disappointed with life, we often stay busy to numb the pain.

Bitterness prevents God's love from filling us, while busyness fills the space with substitutes for genuine hope. Neither permits room for God to move. Isaiah's prophecy to the ancient Israelites deserves a hearing again today:

> See, I am doing a new thing!
>   Now it springs up; do you not perceive it?
> I am making a way in the wilderness
>   and streams in the wasteland.
>   (Isaiah 43:19)

Do you not perceive the fresh outpouring of God's presence upon everyday life? What a challenge for our time. Our experience of his presence grows only when we choose to slow down. One of the great practices this season is the discipline of saying no. Henri Nouwen wrote that in the spiritual life, discipline is "the effort to create some space in which God can act."[6] We must learn to say no so we can say yes to what is better. Slowing down is the pathway to genuine perceiving. God wants to make a way in the wilderness called life and bring refreshment in our exhausted wasteland. Will you prepare him room?

This season, where might God be inviting you specifically, not generally, to say no in order to create space to say yes to pursuits of greater meaning? Augustine once said,

"Why do you want to speak and not want to listen? You are always rushing out of doors but are unwilling to return into your own house. Your teacher is within."[7]

Silence is the path to wonder, and stillness is the way to awe. Maybe this Christmas can be a call to Sabbath from social media, entertainment, and the daily (perhaps hourly) newsfeed. Maybe it's an invitation to spend more time in nature or spiritual reading. Perhaps it's the nudge to wake up a few minutes earlier to savor the silence before the demands of the day set in.

Reflection

Slowly read Luke 1:5–25, and then reflect on the sketch below. What might God be asking you to say no to this season in order to say yes to something better?

5

ELIZABETH: SOLITUDE

The Practice of Hearing God
Luke 1:23–45

THINK BACK TO THE 2020 PANDEMIC. (TOO SOON?)
Amid all the questions people were asking around the globe,
one of the most frequently asked online was, "Why are the
birds so loud?" Seriously. Many people wondered if the pandemic increased the volume level of chirping birds. Bird
expert Sue Anne Zollinger was understandably skeptical. In
fact, she believed that the birds were doing just the opposite.

They were, according to her research at Manchester Metropolitan University, chirping more softly![1] Seriously.

In reality, the noise pollution decreased in the pandemic, so the birds had less noise to compete with to communicate with one another. The human perception was that the chirping became louder, but ironically, it was softer—yet easier to hear because of the relative lack of competing noise.

A spiritual metaphor emerges here to illustrate the story of Elizabeth in Luke's gospel. After learning that she had conceived, she hid in solitude for five months. As with the chirping birds, her capacity to hear God's voice then amplified, leaving us an example to follow in the season of Advent.

Elijah the prophet also heard God's voice amplified as noise levels dissipated. The Scriptures record that God's voice was best heard not in the roaring wind, thunderous earthquake, or tempestuous fire but in the still, small whisper (see 1 Kings 19:11–13). Elijah's capacity to hear God and respond was directly connected to the dissipation of noise through solitude. In solitude, our ability to hear is enhanced. Likewise, Jesus regularly secluded himself to refuel his ministry. Slowing down and seeking solitude is tremendously resourceful. Elizabeth, too, modeled this practice for us. But before we get there, let's explore the text for a few things that have perhaps been overlooked.

When [Zechariah's] time of service was completed, he returned home. After this his wife Elizabeth became pregnant and for five months remained in seclusion.

"The Lord has done this for me," she said. "In these days he has shown his favor and taken away my disgrace among the people." (Luke 1:23–25)

Elizabeth confessed her experience of "disgrace." Social disgrace is traumatic. The Greek word used here is *oneidos,* and this is the only occasion it's utilized in the New Testament. *Oneidos* can mean "disgrace" or "shame." Luke tells us that Elizabeth had felt disgraced among the people (see 1:25). She was physically barren, making her socially broken. Don't miss that. *Oneidos* is applied beyond one's circumstances into their whole character. That's brutal. Elizabeth's barrenness caused public suspicion as to her personal holiness, her marriage, and her entire life. The village gossip must have been ruthless. Both she and Zechariah descended from priestly lineage but, prior to the baby's conception, were probably rumored to be frauds like many of the corrupted Sadducees at the time. *Why else would she be barren?* some probably thought. And if we lived in that time and place, maybe we would have too.

But all those decades of disgrace were then erased in a moment. God fulfilled the word given through the angel Gabriel, and Elizabeth conceived in old age (see verse 24). Yet then Luke revealed a twist in the plot that we should not gloss over. One would imagine the temptation for Elizabeth to run through the streets of her Judean village, proclaiming the news concerning the coming prophet growing in her womb—a kind of "check me out" revenge parade. But she didn't do that. Instead, she "socially distanced" (again, too soon?) and retreated into seclusion (see verse 24). Take a moment to reflect on the sketch below:

The Greek word for "seclusion" (*perikrybo*) is also the word used for "solitude." It literally means to hide oneself. Why would Elizabeth do that?

First, it is possible she wanted to keep her pregnancy quiet until her womb began to show after the fifth month. The social trauma she endured for decades left her reputation in question. Perhaps she feared that if she went public with the news and then miscarried, it might call her character into even greater suspicion. Second, like Mary, she perhaps wanted to ponder the wonder. Not only was it unlikely for a woman to conceive in old age, but the magnitude of her story joining the biblical ranks of Sarah, Rebekah, Rachel, and Hannah must have been humbling. These legendary women also conceived in old age and were viewed as vessels of God's miraculous grace. That's a lot to ponder. Third, in seclusion, Elizabeth and Zechariah would search the Scriptures to understand the significance of their coming son to advance the mission of the coming Messiah.

The story is incredible. For the better part of a lifetime, she felt disgraced; then she was thrust into the center of the biblical narrative. In the blink of an eye, God made broken things new. Isaiah's prophecy was coming true again:

> See, I am doing a new thing!
>> Now it springs up; do you not perceive it?
> I am making a way in the wilderness
>> and streams in the wasteland.
>> (Isaiah 43:19)

For Elizabeth, the desert of barrenness had transformed into a river of legacy. Seclusion—not crowds—became the context where she could ponder the wonder of it all.

THERE AND BACK AGAIN

Luke then whisked the reader north from the hill country of Judea to the village called Nazareth (see Luke 1:26). It is there that Gabriel told Mary that she would carry the Messiah through the miraculous conception by the Holy Spirit. Notice what happened next in the story: "*At that time* Mary got ready and hurried to a town in the hill country of Judea" (verse 39).

Very little time, if any, elapsed between Mary hearing the news of her pregnancy and then heading south to the hill country to visit Elizabeth. The description ("at that time") matters. Every word in the text is meaningful. There was no way for Mary to quickly spread the news of her pregnancy to anyone local, much less to her distant relative Elizabeth. This was the first century. No email, no text, no tweet. Word spread slowly. Mary readied and rushed out the door: "Peace, y'all. Going south. Be back soon."

Mary then arrived at Elizabeth's and was promptly greeted. Nothing in the text indicates Mary blurted out her news. She simply greeted Elizabeth, most likely with the greeting the people of Israel have been using for thousands of years: "Shalom aleichem," which means "Peace unto you." And before Elizabeth could return the greeting ("Aleichem shalom"), baby John leaped in her belly—which makes us wonder how Elizabeth immediately knew Mary was also with child. But Luke already told us the answer before we ask the question . . .

The answer lies in Elizabeth's solitude (see Luke 1:24)!

Like the rising sound of birds in 2020, in solitude Elizabeth's understanding of God's unfolding story expanded. Her (and our) capacity to directly hear God's voice increased in proportion to her willingness to eliminate the noise. She modeled for us the treasures discovered from a private life with God. Through the leaping of Elizabeth's son in utero, the Holy Spirit revealed to Elizabeth that Mary was carrying the promised one to which her child would later point.

The principle for us here is simple: All those who seek God in solitude can expect the indwelling Spirit to impart revelation for life. There are many ways the Spirit speaks to us. Some people hear God most clearly through the Scriptures or creation or art and music or gut impressions about a situation. For others, God speaks clearly through trusted friends or, on occasion, through random strangers (see Hebrews 13:2) or even by billboards! What is vital is that all who have received the Spirit of Christ lack nothing. Yet so many followers of Jesus today do not believe they hear from God—at least not regularly. If you relate to that, you are not alone.

Subconsciously, many pronounce lies over themselves every day:

I'm just an ordinary guy.
I'm just a mom.
I'm just a middle schooler.
I'm just a church attender and I don't know the Bible very well.
Insert your *I'm just* . . . here: _____.

At the time of Jesus, perhaps the greatest lie about one's inability to hear God was this: *I'm just a woman.*

WOMEN AT THE TIME OF JESUS

Let's back up. In the Hebrew Scriptures (also known as the Old Testament), women—including Esther, Deborah, Jael, and others—were empowered by God both inside and outside the home. However, some scholars believe that during the several hundred years between the Old and New Testaments (often referred to as the intertestamental period), women were confined to the home and viewed as the inferior gender. We deduce this from circulated writings of a Jewish scribe in Jerusalem named Ben Sira during the early second century B.C. Although his "wisdom" taught that women could be good wives and mothers and are to be respected, he encouraged men to adhere to the following:

> Women are responsible for sin coming into the world and their spite is unbearable. (Sir 25:13–26)

> Deed no property to her during your lifetime and do not let her support you. (Sir 33:20; 25:22–26)

> If you don't like your wife, don't trust her. (Sir 7:26)

> Be careful to keep records of the supplies you issue to her. (Sir 42:6–7)[2]

It is important to note that the *Wisdom of Ben Sira* was enculturated in conservative Jewish homes by the time of Jesus. What precisely motivated Ben Sira is unclear, but we can say with certainty that his wisdom was often used by others to suppress women. Sira believed that "daughters are a disaster."[3] Hebrew scholar Kenneth Bailey noted that "with the passage of time and the rise of the rabbinic movement, the position of women by New Testament times was, on all levels, inferior to men."[4]

Imagine hearing the following from Luke's gospel in a male-dominated society in the first century, a time when Ben Sira's opinion on women was commonly held: "Elizabeth was filled with the Holy Spirit" (Luke 1:41).

Luke's words here are significant—revolutionary even—because in the first century, gender roles were deeply entrenched. But among the first people in the New Testament (written by males, mind you) to be filled with the Holy Spirit were neither priests nor rabbis, neither males nor scribes. Rather, they were women! Luke was clear from the onset that Mary and Elizabeth were filled with God's Spirit. The Gospels demonstrate that participants in God's kingdom are not excluded based on categories such as gender and race. Instead, the Spirit fills vessels of least resistance—those who seek God with all their hearts.

Elizabeth and Mary were among the first to experience the Holy Spirit in the New Testament. In the last chapter of Luke's gospel, we're told that women were also the first to witness the Resurrection and spread the good news. This is huge! God delights to speak to whoever will listen. In solitude, God redirects our attention. Women are just as capable to hear God as men are. At the time of Jesus, that would not have been expected. The kingdom of God is full of surprises. God is always better than we think.

You might find yourself wondering, *Why would God speak to me? I'm not qualified!* Well, guess what: "Being willing to do what you are not qualified to do is sometimes what qualifies you."[5] If God once spoke to and through a donkey (see Numbers 22:28–31), why would he not also speak to and through *you*? Advent is an invitation to slow, to still, and to seek solitude to hear God's whisper over you. Can you make some room for that this season?

What began in solitude overflowed in community. Elizabeth's private life with God in solitude eventually led her to rejoice in praise with Mary:

> In a loud voice [Elizabeth] exclaimed: "Blessed are you among women, and blessed is the child you will bear!" (Luke 1:42)

The kingdom life is deeply personal, but it's never only private. God's personal revelation draws us into fellowship and praise with others. Elizabeth has much to teach us who live in an individualistic age.

GATHERINGS ARE MEANT FOR GATHERING

Years ago, I was guest preaching at a church in New Jersey. Before the gathering, many of us were talking in the back of the sanctuary. Natural light was pouring in through the windows. All of a sudden, the curtains were drawn and the light extinguished. In a room of darkness, we made our way toward the seats. The stage lit up and the fog poured out. The band emerged and the music began. I didn't feel excited; instead, a touch of sadness entered my soul. We had come to be together—to belong and grow as a community. Yet as we worshipped in that room, amid the darkness and fog, it didn't feel communal; it felt lonely. I couldn't hear our voices singing praise to God; instead, they were drowned out by the monitor's decibels.

Elizabeth and Mary experienced the opposite when they came together. They each had encountered God in solitude, and then they came together as a community of praise. When we, the church, gather for worship, we are bringing together all the moments of solitude with God we've experienced throughout the week and collectively praising God for what he has done. The gathered worship of the church shouldn't drown out our voices and make us feel alone; it should do just the opposite, actually. The gathering of praise between Elizabeth and Mary was a foretaste of the gathered church. Jesus would later say to his disciples, "What is whispered in your ear, proclaim from the roofs" (Matthew 10:27). God's whispers in solitude lead us to shouts of praise in community.

What if we can hear God better than we think? In solitude, we can. We then bring what he has done in our solitude into the gathered community for praise.

Reflection

Read Luke 1:23–45, and then reflect on the sketch below. What might God be asking of you that you have been avoiding or suppressing?

JOHN THE BAPTIST: WONDER

The Practice of Believing Absurdity

Luke 1:39–80

I'VE NEVER BEEN PREGNANT, BUT I'M TOLD THE EX-
perience is so profound that expectant women bond together
more easily than they do with those not expecting. More
than two thousand years ago, a unique meetup occurred between two pregnant women named Elizabeth and Mary.
Elizabeth carried a son named John, who would become a
great prophet and rabbi. Mary carried a son named Jesus,

the Messiah for whom the world had waited. Luke tells us that the introduction of John with Jesus—mediated through their godly mothers—was so intense that the Holy Spirit caused the baby inside the womb of Elizabeth to leap. For John, the moment marked the launch of a life spent pointing in the direction of Jesus. Jesus would be the point of his life.

In 2012, my wife, Elaina, and I were expecting our daughter, Eloise. That year, an irresistible app for pregnant parents seeking to chart their baby's growth in utero hit the market. The strangest (and most appealing) feature of the app is that it compares a baby's development to the size of fruits and vegetables. For example, when our daughter was twenty-four weeks in utero, the app informed us that she was the size of a rutabaga. So cool. *You go, Little Ruty!*

At thirty-two weeks, she had grown to the size of a jicama. (I had to look up what that was.) I mention this because when John first met Jesus (in utero), John was somewhere between the size of a rutabaga and a jicama, and Jesus was about the size of a lentil. Trust me: This is going somewhere.

JICAMA JOHN

In the presence of Jesus, John performed gymnastic-like leaps in the womb:

> When Elizabeth heard Mary's greeting, the baby *leaped* in her womb. (Luke 1:41)

Why did Luke include the detail about the baby leaping? Rationally, it's absurd to think John could possess any knowledge whatsoever about metaphysical truths at that stage in his little (unborn) life. Surely, Luke knew this. Maybe absurdity was, in fact, his point. Luke began his gospel in absurd fashion to remind us that God's ways are not often our ways. Our rational brains are wonderful, but they cannot fully comprehend the mysteriousness of God's movements. Our ability to reason is a gift, but our brains can never contain the wonders of his love.

At the time of his leap, even though unborn John was about the size of a jicama, he recognized and responded to the presence of the Messiah. Slow down and think about this: What are we to make of it? One baby in utero leaping at the presence of another baby in utero. Have you ever heard a sermon on it? I haven't. It's tempting to slide past this verse and move on in the story as if that were totally normal. Only it wasn't normal. It was anything but.

So, let's resist the urge to move quickly and instead pause to wonder and prod. Anatomically speaking, at six months in utero, John was beginning to open his tiny eyelids for the first time. But it's not like he could see Jesus from the womb. Further, John's brain was nowhere near capable of cognitive discernment, particularly around spiritual questions like, *Is this the Messiah?* or *What is truth?* or *Would I prefer my mother to order ceviche or short-rib gnocchi for dinner?*

Nevertheless, Jicama John leaped in recognition of the Messiah—who, again, was about the size of a lentil. And although his eyelids were just then opening, John saw and recognized Jesus with a different kind of sight. Isn't that absurd? There is nothing rational about this story. Luke's gospel does not fit comfortably within the postmodern plausibility structures. So, how do we reconcile John's little leap of faith with the Enlightenment worldview that has shaped Western civilization for the past four hundred years? The story Luke told leads us to a fork in the spiritual road: Either we reject the absurdity outright, or we ponder it, seeking to expand our understanding.

Maybe the Scriptures are deeper than we are. Maybe they see more than we do. Maybe they know truth better than we do.

THE ENLIGHTENMENT

Though many people today might cling to postmodern relativism (the theory that truth is subjective, based on an individual's perspective), our age still draws heavily from the Enlightenment (the theory that truth is objective for everyone, everywhere). Several hundred years ago, Western civilization was (re)built on a rational foundation, which produced many influential—and mostly European—thinkers who proposed that all truth must be observable and describable. In other words, only what can be observed and described through the five major senses can be verified as truth.

So, how does John's little leap in the womb fit into this cultural worldview? It doesn't. We have no category for this. Therefore, we are left with the choice to reject and discard it or expand and receive it. Some have attempted to forge a middle path by metaphorizing the miraculous stories in Scripture, but that usually leaves us with more questions than answers.

If we hold to Enlightenment theory (and the subsequent scientific method) as to what may be qualified as truth, we must discard the story, because none of John's senses were engaged (except perhaps half-opened eyelids). For starters, the babies were in separate wombs. Further, John could not smell, touch, or hear the lentil-sized Jesus when Mary greeted Elizabeth. But Luke tells us he leaped anyway. But how could he leap if he had not yet developed the cognitive ability to process and recognize truth, much less receive it? That is the question! And that is what Luke wants us to ponder.

All this leads us to wonder, Is there a path of spiritual knowing—of deeper sight than what our eyeballs can perceive—that lies deeper than our cognitive reasoning? Is it possible to know that something is true beyond the categories of Enlightenment theory?

Perhaps Jicama John perceived something deeper than the kind of knowledge that comes only from rational human cognition. And maybe we can know truth at a deeper level than sensory experience. It's as if the Holy Spirit imparted a sixth sense to John that the theory of Enlightenment did not factor into its doctrines. The Christian faith has a term for this: *revelation*. Revelation does not dismiss rational categories of truth, but it is willing to transcend these created categories.

Are you beginning to see why you've never heard a sermon on this topic?

REASON OF THE HEART

What am I saying here? First, God is not opposed to the rational, reasonable mind. He made it. He created a coherent universe. Christian faith does not conflict with science. Christian faith does conflict with naturalism. Defined by Roger Olson, "Naturalism is the worldview that presupposes that nature is all that exists, which is a belief not proven or sustained by science, even if many scientists have adopted it."[1]

God is not contained by human categories of knowledge. He existed long before creation and even longer before the age of Enlightenment. God does not check in with the human rules of physics before acting in the world. Claims of the Christian faith often rise above reason, but those claims are not beneath some measure of logic. For example, the tomb of Christ really was (and is) empty. Christians believe that is because Jesus is risen. Reason will not lead you to draw that conclusion (far from it, actually), but when all the evidence is considered, it is a logical option. You don't have to check your brain at the door to follow (or leap toward) Jesus.

God loves the mind, but John's leap teaches us that sometimes God moves in ways beyond reason. The great scientist Blaise Pascal was right: "The heart has its reasons of which reason knows nothing. . . . We know the truth not only through our reason but also through our heart."[2] Many have said that the mind is a wonderful servant but terrible master. This rings true particularly in the Christmas season.

Some are waiting for God to fully make sense to their rational minds before they believe. I'm all for discernment, but limiting an eternal God to fit nicely into our recently formed human categories is perhaps more absurd than John's leap.

Think of it this way: Do we force romance to adhere rationally? Hardly. When I fell in love with Elaina, I didn't first check with the scientific method. No one does. And if they do, run! The "knowledge" from which I drew to pursue and commit my life to her was felt deep in my gut. To describe the phenomenon, we use language such as "fell in love." Why? Because it is like a leap we make without thinking about it. Truth can be recognized at levels deeper than in our minds. That doesn't make truth subjective, but it does make it deeper than just cognition.

When I first became aware of God's presence in middle school, I didn't pause to consult the tenets of the Enlightenment. I *sensed,* if you will, that the story of God's profound love for the world—and for me—is true. And the invitation was to take a leap to follow Jesus. We can know things at levels deeper than reason.

Years ago, while pastoring in Southern California, I had an intelligent young parishioner approach me and say, "John leaping inside a womb, the virgin birth . . . Come on, AJ, do we really still believe all this? Didn't we disprove God's existence in the eighties?"

We did, in fact, disprove some things in the 1980s. We disproved that Peter Cetera was better off without Chicago. We disproved that the Walkman was a perennial appendage. We disproved that hair crimping was here to stay. We didn't, however, disprove that *Back to the Future* may be the best film of all time. And that decade certainly did not disprove God's existence or the virgin birth or even John's leap.

The Scriptures teach us that God can be known through human cognition. The slow conversion story of Nicodemus over the course of John's gospel is proof of this. But God is also a being who does not submit to human categories of knowledge, helpful as they may be. When the Holy Spirit acts—even within a womb, when we are like vegetables of various sizes—our theories, philosophies, and reason cannot contain how God's revelation flows to human hearts. And in response, we sometimes take a leap.

EXPANDING OUR UNDERSTANDING

To be clear, God is not calling the church to stupidity or to checking our minds at the door or to questioning gravity or the molecular structure of boron. Rather, God is inviting us into a sacred imagination where our knowledge can expand to make room for wonder. That is what the season of Advent is entirely about. In our waiting, God expands us. It is always a mistake—honest or otherwise—to reduce his capabilities to our level of comprehension. For those who seek a vibrant spiritual life, the minimum entry requirement is the willingness to suspend disbelief long enough to ponder new possibilities.

Lewis Carroll's famous work *Through the Looking Glass*

captures well the essence of John's leap and the sacred imagination we are called into at Advent:

> "I can't believe *that!*" said Alice.
>
> "Can't you?" the Queen said in a pitying tone. "Try again: draw a long breath and shut your eyes."
>
> Alice laughed. "There's no use trying," she said. "One *can't* believe impossible things."
>
> "I daresay you haven't had much practice," said the Queen. "When I was your age, I always did it for half-an-hour a day. Why, sometimes I've believed as many as six impossible things before breakfast."[3]

Around this time of year, many pause to wonder if there is a grander faith story to provide identity, purpose, coherence, and meaning. "The simple reality of life," according to scientist and theologian Alister McGrath, "is that all of us, irrespective of our views about God, base our lives on beliefs on things that we cannot prove to be true, but believe to be trustworthy and reliable. . . . [Belief is] not blind; it just tries to make the best sense of things on the basis of the limited evidence available."[4]

The Enlightenment taught us to *understand in order to believe.* Fair enough. In some categories of life, that is a wise approach. But in the spiritual life, that is not what the ancients taught us. Among countless other individuals, Anselm of Canterbury offered us the Latin phrase *credo ut intelligam:* "I believe in order to understand." That way of thinking is the exact opposite of modern understanding. Our ancestors thought that understanding was gained and expanded only through a leap of faith, not solely through reason. Maybe that was the leap John was making—a leap that started a movement. John's leap shows us that we don't need to first figure out every mystery in our brains. If we could, it would no longer be faith. Instead, the faith of Christ is a pathway of being figured out: Credo ut intelligam. We don't understand and then believe. Rather, by believing (or trusting, or trying on), we begin to understand that it's all

> because of the tender mercy of our God,
>> by which the rising sun will come to us
>>> from heaven
> to shine on those living in darkness
>> and in the shadow of death,
> to guide our feet into the path of peace.
>> (Luke 1:78–79)

POINTING THE FINGER

Some uncles give you socks for Christmas. Mine once gave me a cruise down the Rhine. His previously planned trip was set to expire, so he generously invited Elaina and me to take his now unwanted expedition. Humbly and happily, we accepted. On the second-to-last day, the cruise ported in Alsace, France, where the stork serves as the region's most iconic symbol. Fitting for this chapter, I think. That morning, while enjoying my black coffee and poached eggs, I consulted the map before leaving the boat. At that moment, a mental lightbulb turned on. Eureka! Our port was just minutes outside Colmar, France. Colmar is a town that houses Matthias Grünewald's *Isenheim Altarpiece*—a painting of John the Baptist, no longer jicama-sized, in a unique and profound pose. So I ditched my previously made plans for the day and hailed a taxi to the Unterlinden Museum. I even convinced some friends on the cruise to join me.

In the center of the altarpiece hangs a crucified Jesus, gaunt and discolored. To his left is a colorful John the Baptist, pointing a long and bony finger at Christ as if to say, *He is the way; follow him.* It may seem odd that Grünewald painted John the Baptist into a scene that occurred after he was beheaded. But John knew that the Lamb of God, born of Mary, was destined to die for the sin of the world (see

John 1:29). John spent his life directing people to the "knowledge of salvation," as prophesied by his father, Zechariah:

> You, my child, will be called a prophet of the
>   Most High;
>   for you will go on before the Lord to prepare
>   the way for him,
> to give his people the knowledge of salvation
>   through the forgiveness of their sins.
>   (Luke 1:76–77)

Notice the phrase "knowledge of salvation." Jesus, a common name in the first century, was the Greek form of Joshua. His name means "the Lord is salvation."[5] To know Jesus is to know salvation, because he is the relational embodiment of what humans need most. The knowledge of salvation here isn't a systematic theology, confessional document, or unifying creed. Zechariah prophesied that Jesus himself is the salvation the world is looking for. This kind of knowledge is relational before it is rational. It's a form of knowledge that is incarnational. It is revelation—not cognition—that made baby John leap in the womb.

John's life provokes in us the question *Where does your life point?* Pardon the wordplay, but what is the *point* of your life? No matter your industry, season of parenting, stage of retirement, or year as a student, your life always points to something. Since Genesis 3, our fingers naturally invert to refer back to ourselves. Sometimes we are tempted to turn our middle fingers upward while looking at someone else. Your life will always aim toward something. As with John, our lives take on greatest significance when we point beyond ourselves to the Son of God.

The call of John was to draw our attention to the first coming of Christ: the Lamb of God. The call of the church is to draw our attention to the second coming of Christ: the King of kings. Jesus, who is salvation, was the Lamb of God and will return as the King of creation. We live in the Second Advent, awaiting Christ to be all in all. He is coming. What is the point of your life?

Reflection

Read Luke 1:41, and then reflect on the sketch below. As you do, ask yourself, When has God moved me to respond?

GABRIEL: NOTICING

The Practice of Welcoming Angels

Luke 1:26–38

I OFTEN WONDER IF THE WORLD IS PROFOUNDLY enchanted with God's presence. Long ago, Jacob confessed, "The LORD is in this place, and I was not aware of it" (Genesis 28:16). Declarations like these haunt me, in the best of ways.

Every year, I lead a group of willing pilgrims to the Near East where Jesus declared and demonstrated the kingdom of God. While in the land, we walk, study, pray, and feast. Jerusalem is marked by limestone architecture and tree-covered hills against a skyline of desert brown. During the first trip I led, because our hotel was furnished with balconies, I was able to gaze over Jerusalem every day. But I assumed that the iconic Dome of the Rock, situated on the Temple Mount, was out of my view, tucked somewhere behind the hilltops and inaccessible to the eye from my location.

I began and concluded each day in the same way: praying and reading from my balcony. On our final evening in Jerusalem, my friend Jay joined me for dinner on my perch overlooking the city. As we reflected and relived stories from our past, I saw something familiar and wondered aloud, "Is that the Mount of Olives?" The Mount of Olives is now a sand-colored hillside lined with thousands of graves. It slopes down into what we call the Garden of Gethsemane.

Squinting, I peered at a tree-grown hilltop. Whoa! Between the trees, I could faintly see the golden dome—the Dome of the Rock—glistening in the sunset. To my friend's surprise, I exclaimed, "We are looking at the site of Jesus's Triumphal Entry!" And, like Jacob, I confessed, "It's been there the whole time, and I was not aware."

ENCHANTED EARTH

Maybe there is much more to reality than meets the everyday eye. Perhaps the Bible's inclusion of angelic beings throughout its entirety is evidence of this. What if the world is charged with far more spiritual activity than we notice?

Borrowing a word from the philosopher Charles Taylor, what if the earth is *enchanted* with heaven?[1] Like Jacob, perhaps on the other side of life we will discover that many things—visible and invisible—were ever-present and we were unaware. Perhaps.

Angels saturate the Christmas story as extensions of God's indwelling presence. Angels—not humans—were also first to announce the good news of Christ's birth. And their proclamation was made to poor shepherds, not the wealthy and powerful elite. Angels throughout the Bible were "help from heaven."[2] If you've ever received insight into a problem or felt oddly protected from harm or sensed a vague spiritual nudge toward a specific direction, maybe the Lord's angelic emissaries were there and you were unaware.[3]

In her book *Walking on Water,* the great writer Madeleine L'Engle observed, "We lose our ability to see angels as we grow up."[4] By this, she didn't mean that age inhibits our vision; she meant we live in a culture that encourages us to suppress our imaginations as we age. We do this in the name of cultural sophistication. We think it is charming to believe in (and claim to see) angels as little children. But as we grow, we are encouraged to put this enchanted nonsense behind us.

For all the gifts of the Enlightenment, its greatest liability was confining possibilities beyond what we can see through a microscope. Jesus once said that adults would do well to become like children if they are to enter the kingdom (see Matthew 18:3). Maybe Jesus wasn't talking about a future kingdom that will one day manifest. Maybe he also meant that the kingdom is now in our midst but we no longer have eyes to see it.

No wonder God then sent Gabriel to a young girl (see Luke 1:26–38). This virgin would believe and receive the angel's good news. Notice that when Gabriel visited the religious old man named Zechariah, he had a more difficult time believing and receiving the good news (see verses 11–20).

L'Engle was right. We must be aware that as we age, we can lose our ability to spiritually see. We slowly close our souls to everything that cannot be scientifically explained. I still hear the sweet voice of Louis Armstrong singing all the lyrics leading up to "And I think to myself, what a wonderful world."[5] Beautiful and true as the song may be, the lyrics of this entire song capture the beauty of life available to only the senses, observable to the fields of science. But what if even greater beauty and wonder lies also beyond the senses, waiting to be perceived? If an angel visited you today (in a dream or in a stranger or in a vision), would you be open to believing? Or would you explain it away?

ENCHANTED BIBLE

From Genesis to Revelation, angels saturate the narrative. Gabriel's angelic presence on earth was not an outlier; Gabriel was perhaps the norm made manifest. What more can we say? A lot.

In the story of Abraham, angels became his guests (see Genesis 18:2). Jacob wrestled with an angel all night (see 32:24). Through an angel, Daniel was given political wisdom (see Daniel 10:10–14). John the Revelator fell prostrate after an angel visited him on the island of Patmos (see Revelation 1:1). Angels gave directions to lowly shepherds under the evening sky (see Luke 2:8–9). Angels ministered to Jesus in the desert after he vanquished Satan, an angel of darkness (see Matthew 4:1). According to Jesus, he could have called more than twelve legions of angels to his aid on the cross if he so desired (see Matthew 26:53). And, of course, there is the mysterious line in the book of Hebrews that encourages all of us to practice hospitality, because the ones we serve may, in fact, be angels (again, refer to Hebrews 13:2). According to the Scriptures, angels could be anywhere. In the Bible, we see them everywhere.

But here's the question: Do you live as if this is true? I don't. I could rightfully be accused of living many of my days in a world devoid of divine presence. Perhaps we occasionally hear testimonies of angel visitations or God moments or the Holy Spirit coming down in a worship gathering. But experiencing God's presence as occasionally available on earth is *not* the worldview of the Bible. A plain reading of Scripture reveals that angels fill the whole earth, and I want to live as if I believe that. The season of Advent means to help us to reclaim this.

Maybe the possibility of enchantment—that there is more than meets the eye—explains why fantasy authors like Tolkien, Lewis, and Rowling grip us with their stories. Perhaps even the staunchest of atheists long to believe that there is more at play in the world than meets the eye. I think most people would like to believe that the world is permeated with a presence greater than us. Perhaps angelic beings are present through a hidden dimension or alternate frequency. Maybe we inhabit a God-saturated earth, one where the Creator is always and ever *with us.*

L'Engle reflected on the many angelic encounters from Scripture, suggesting,

> All the angelic host as they are described in Scripture, have a wild and radiant power that often takes us by surprise. They are not always gentle. They bar the entrance to Eden so that we may never return home. They send plagues upon the Egyptians. They are messengers of God. They are winds. They are flames of fire. They are young men dressed in white.[6]

It is no wonder that a glimpse of Gabriel sent shivers up Mary's spine. To believe the Bible is to believe in angels. Sorry, secular humanism, but the world is enchanted with divine presence, chock-full of God stuff. Just as Jacob's ladder found angels ascending and descending (see Genesis 28:12), the realm of the heavens and earth intricately overlap. Therefore, the question is not *Where is God's presence?* The better question is *Where isn't God's presence?* That was David's meditation in Psalm 139. As oxygen fills the lungs, God's presence invisibly permeates the cosmos, providing an enduring lifeline to the soul even when we cannot see.

RAINBOW WI-FI

What if Wi-Fi were visible? Experts suggest the rainbow-colored electromagnetic signals and radio waves would barrage us. It has been claimed that our senses would be crushed by the overall amount of visual input.[7] If that invisible reality is true of something human beings created, how much more possible might the constant presence of divine light and energy all around us be?

Contrary to popular opinion, every human being believes in the invisible every day. I mean, one of the first things we do when checking into a hotel is ask the concierge, "What's the Wi-Fi password?"

I often wonder if the kingdom of God is like a frequency that some people are tapped into while others are not. Jesus seemingly operated at a deeper level of connection with the Father than did those around him. I'm less convinced that Jesus had special access and now suspect he was simply more attuned to what is always here yet often hidden from plain sight. One time, the Pharisees asked him about when the kingdom would come. He replied,

> The coming of the kingdom of God is not something that can be observed, nor will people say, "Here it is," or "There it is," because the kingdom of God is in your midst. (Luke 17:20–21)

That sounds like frequency language—like Jesus is aware of hidden dimensions of reality that are ever-present and available. To access the kingdom, then, requires faith where we cannot see.

The kingdom is not "out there" somewhere beyond the blue. Nor is it merely waiting for us in the future when we die. Although we await the kingdom to fully arrive "on earth as it is in heaven" (Matthew 6:10), Jesus reminds us that the kingdom is also in our midst. This means that, in some form or another, it is available to us.

The other day, I was stopped next to another car at a red light. We were both blaring our radios but had them set to different stations. With reference to the kingdom, it dawned on me that two people can be in the exact same place while tuned in to different frequencies. That is what Jesus meant, I think. When we tune our hearts, quiet our souls, and live with the story of Scripture open before us, we can see and live at a deeper level of reality. Jesus said, "He can do only what he sees his Father doing" (John 5:19). He lived at a deeper frequency and is inviting us this Advent to slow down and do likewise.

POSITIONS AND POSTURES

In the ancient world, dreams were commonly thought to be vehicles of God's revelation.[8] In Matthew's gospel alone, angels appear through dreams at least six times (1:20; 2:12, 13, 19, 22; 27:19). How profound that angels spoke not only to Jewish men such as Joseph but also to pagan women such as Pilate's wife! God is everywhere (including in our sleep) and is desirous to speak with anyone open to listening, even those outside the faith.

Gabriel spoke to Zechariah and Mary on different occasions. He was the same angel who visited the prophet Daniel hundreds of years before (see Daniel 8). The man was in a deep sleep when he encountered Gabriel and was terrified in his presence. After their encounter, "Daniel . . . was worn out [and] lay exhausted for several days" (verse 27). Perhaps it's God's provision that we are not yet fully aware of his omnipresence. Maybe, like with Wi-Fi, the overall visual input would crush us in our current state.

According to the Bible, angels speak. What humans choose to do with their instruction bears tremendous impact on our lives. It did with Zechariah, and it certainly did with Mary. The key difference between Gabriel's visits with Zechariah and ones with Mary was a posture of openness. After Gabriel spoke, both Zechariah and Mary asked follow-up questions. We should never interpret from Scripture that God is opposed to our questions. He knows we are finite beings. However, he is opposed to a posture of narrow-mindedness. When we limit the possibilities of God's revelation, our hearts close in. Remember Zechariah, how he was silenced, not as punishment but as an invitation to be still and open to new possibilities. Therefore, the nine-month silencing of Zechariah prepared in him an expanded capacity for spiritual imagination. Mary, in stark contrast, immediately replied, "Behold, I am the servant of the Lord; let it be to me according to your word" (Luke 1:38, ESV).

Notice two significant things:

1. Mary's *position:* "I am the servant," thus, not the Lord. Unlike what we find in much of secular humanism today, Mary does not perceive herself as the one in control who gets to determine possibilities.

2. Mary's *posture:* "Let it be to me according to *your* word" and, thus, not according to *her* worldview. She holistically offers herself for God's will to be done. Mary submits to God's revelation through Gabriel and offers herself in surrendered obedience.

Mary modeled for us one who accesses the kingdom of God. God's activity was made clear to her because she continually opened herself to new possibilities. Mary was the image of what faithful discipleship looks like. Those individuals desirous to notice God more in everyday life would do well to follow her position of servant and her posture of surrender.

ANGELS UNAWARE

Let's continue to ponder the question *What if the world is enchanted far more than we think?* The writer of Hebrews encourages us with the news that there is a cloud of witnesses (dead saints) who surround us from another dimension (see 12:1). Why, then, not angels too? What if Jacob was right that the Lord is here and we are unaware?

Perhaps life is about peering long and deep enough on the balcony to perceive that what we are searching for is hidden in plain sight. Maybe angels surround us every second of the day but exist in frequencies just beyond our noticing. I'm curious how an increase of spiritual awareness to the presence of God—angels or otherwise—might affect our daily lives. I'm curious if we, too (like Mary), might become full of God's empowering grace if our posture became that of servants and our position took the form of surrender.

Whatever the case may be, the author of Hebrews inspires us to take angels seriously. They are like ladders from God that connect heaven and earth, and we should live with the possibility of their presence in mind and not forget to show hospitality to all. In the season of Christmas, God's name is Immanuel, meaning that God is with us. Therefore, despite the way we may at times feel, we have never been alone, we never are, and we never will be. God's presence saturates the entire cosmos.

I'm not exactly sure who to talk to about this, nor do I have any skill in songwriting, but perhaps with this chapter in mind, we could have persuaded the late and great Louis Armstrong to insert one additional verse to his iconic song (which you may sing to yourself):

> I see angels sing
> Miracles too
> The earth is imbued
> And being renewed
> And I think to myself,
> What a wonderful world.

What a wonderful world, indeed!

Reflection

From cover to cover, the Scriptures reveal that the presence of God saturates the cosmos. Slowly read and reflect on Luke 1:28, and then spend some time meditating on the sketch below, wondering, What difference would it make in my life to reclaim the presence of God over every moment?

Part 2

CHRISTMAS
The Gift of Receiving

✳

L ike an ocean wave, Advent expectation crescendos swiftly onto the shores of Christmas morning. Immanuel has come; God is with us. The beginning of Christmas marks the conclusion of Advent, and the fruit of Advent is the birth of Christ. Since the year A.D. 336, the church has marked December 25 as the day to keep the feast of Christmas. Joy to the world!

My Christmas Day, like many days, begins early. The gospel is read, the gifts are unwrapped, we feast wholeheartedly, and by afternoon we settle in for "a long winter's nap."[1] It's glorious, really. But by December 26, we begin adjusting our minds and hearts to the secular calendar. January 1, the secular New Year, closes in. Some people turn toward football (if in America) or *fútbol* (if anywhere else in the world), while others get a jump on a resolution or goals for the year ahead.

But be careful. Author and pastor Brian Zahnd wisely cautioned us, "The birth of Messiah is far too big an event to celebrate for a mere day."[2] The party is meant to continue. And the party is not about sports or goals but about salvation. It's not about our resolutions; it's about our transformation. Saint Francis believed that the real gift of Christmas is so spectacular that we should celebrate for days on end! Christmas Day is not the climax of the salvation celebration; it's only the beginning. Let us keep the feast!

Across many Christian traditions, the season of Christmas lingers for twelve full days—not one day, but twelve! More than being the subject of a clever song, these twelve days of Christmas are historically referred to as Christmastide. Although *tide* originally meant "good news" ("glad tidings"), imagery of the ocean tide is poetically useful here as well. Like the Advent season, the celebration of Christmas is not merely a day. Like the continuous tides on the shores of the ocean, the coming of God in Jesus of Nazareth continues to lap onto the shores of our lives again and again and again. Jesus seeks to keep coming to us. He is also the one we believe will return to reign eternally on earth (see Revelation 22:20). On December 26, our lives are not meant to *move on* but to prepare room for Christ to more fully *move in*. In light of this, do you revel in the twelve days of Christmas, or do you quickly move past the sacred to embrace a secular vision?

In 1951, American composer and flutist Meredith Willson wrote the classic song "It's Beginning to Look a Lot Like Christmas." In it, he envisions the season of Christmas with copious amounts of candy canes, a tree in the Grand Hotel, holly on the front door, and toys in every store (specifically, hopalong boots, pistols that shoot, and dolls that talk). The vision of Christmas this song portrays lives deep in the heart of Americans today. But I am confident that Christians prior to the twentieth century would not comprehend such a vision of the coming of Immanuel. I am not suggesting there is no place to include pieces of Willson's vision, but it is important to notice how Christmas has been culturally re-imagined over the past century.[3] We are far more familiar with the songs of Bing Crosby than with Mary's Magnificat.

Some have since suggested there is a war on Christmas. If true, it isn't so much a war on *words* as much as a war on *worlds*. The Gospels draw our imaginations into an ancient world of Christmas with simple humility (manger), sacrificial generosity (Magi), and divine mercy (Immanuel). By contrast, society draws our imaginations into a world of Christmas through images of frenzy ("silver lanes aglow"), consumerism ("toys"), and sugar ("candy canes"). This is a war that's engaging mind, heart, and body. And we've yet to mention the global distraction and giver of good gifts referred to as Santa Claus!

But let's not get carried away or surprised by what is transpiring in our culture with regard to Christmas. After all, though the kingdom is *for* this world, Jesus's kingdom is not *of* this world (see John 18:36). Christ and his kingdom will not be discovered from the forces at work within it. Just as Jesus descended from a different realm and came to the earth, the kingdom will too. The Christian's mission this season is not to crusade against secular images invading the season, crowding out the biblical story at the local mall or the public school. Nor is it to lament how "dark" the world has become and shrink back in fear and victimhood. Rather, in an increasingly secular age, Christmas is a season to once again proclaim humbly but boldly that joy has come to the world—that true Light has come to dispel the artificial lights hanging from the tree.

Christians, therefore, should not be angered by the removal of the word *Christmas* in the public square. When you stop and think about it, replacing the word *Christmas* with *holidays* isn't the problem some people have made it out to be. First, the root of *holidays* is "holy days." Second, notice how the word is plural. The plural form of holidays reminds us that the celebration of the Incarnation extends for days beyond December 25. Twelve days, to be exact![4]

Let's return to the question at hand: Do you revel in the twelve days of Christmas, or do you quickly move past the sacred to embrace a secular vision?

The second section of this book invites us to journey with ancient companions who were the first to experience Immanuel. Some received him, while others rejected him. The same choice remains for every person today. On which side will you find yourself? This Christmas season, will you permit room in your life for Immanuel to further move in? Or will you, like much of society, quickly move on? Here are some invitations to consider as you continue your journey from the Advent vision of active waiting to the Christmas season of joyful receiving:

1. Now that Christmas is here, consider making a schedule to read each of the chapters that follow.
2. Begin each reading with the lighting of a candle as a symbol of inviting Christ, the true Light, to illumine your path.
3. Conclude each chapter by reflecting on the provided sketch for three to five minutes, asking God to fill your imagination with fresh faith and application.
4. Commit to worshipping with a local church body that prizes Jesus above all else.
5. Enjoy food, friendship, and creation in a way that honors and celebrates that joy has come to the world.
6. Keep Christmas decorations displayed for twelve days after Christmas as a symbol to keep the feast.
7. Always remember that "the Word became flesh and made his dwelling among us. We have seen his glory, the glory of the one and only Son, who came from the Father, full of grace and truth" (John 1:14).

SHEPHERDS: CHOSEN

The Practice of Being Found

Luke 2:8–18

"THE LORD IS MY SHEPHERD, I LACK NOTHING." To the everyday Christian, this opening line from Psalm 23 is among the most familiar in the Bible. In the next verse, the psalmist leads us into "green pastures," where a shepherd guides the sheep to graze and safely lie down. What do you imagine the scene looks like? Perhaps you see a shepherd and his sheep dancing down the verdant slopes with Julie

Andrews and the children from *The Sound of Music*. Or maybe your mind goes to lush grasses on the English countryside. I grew up in the valley of Middle Tennessee. When I read this psalm, I visualize the rolling-hill farms on the outskirts of Nashville.

But are these images of lush green grasses what the shepherds of the Bible experienced? Is this the picture we are supposed to imagine when reading Psalm 23? Inescapably, we read the Bible through our own context. Therefore, Christians in the western hemisphere seldom imagine the setting that the writers of Scripture were experiencing. Would you believe me if I told you that these green pastures from Psalm 23 looked very little like the English countryside and were actually arid, brown, and dusty? Sheep would graze on the earthy slopes of the Judean wilderness. Instead of picturing the lush grasses on rolling farms, imagine little sprigs of green sparsely popping up from the soil. The shepherd would lead the sheep to feast on desert hillsides where there was just enough grass to get the flock through the day. Jesus hinted at this notion when he invited his disciples to pray for "daily bread" (Matthew 6:11). In God's mercy, we are often given just enough that we may learn to abide in him and not rely on the illusion that we are self-sufficient. When we, like these sheep, follow God—the Good Shepherd—we lack nothing.

So, what's the point? you might be wondering. Things aren't always what we imagine them to be. That is true not only for the setting of the psalmist's green pastures but also for the vocation of shepherds. For us to understand the significance of shepherds being among the first to witness the birth of Christ, we need to see with new lenses that are both ancient and Near Eastern. When we do this, the seeming oddity of God's choosing shepherds will come into clear focus.

A TRUE STORY

When reading the Nativity story from the Gospels, it is important to remember that the Bible is telling a true story. Luke's gospel functions not as fable but as fact. His account is written as if it really happened—because it did. And it happened in a specific place at a certain time in history. Unlike the settings of Hogwarts in *Harry Potter* and Middle-earth from *The Lord of the Rings,* Bethlehem is a real place, located next to the Judean wilderness.

Nor is the story of Christmas just a feel-good film. Luke informs the reader that the shepherds determined to "go to Bethlehem" (2:15) and that they were keeping watch nearby. It was, therefore, highly likely that the men were just outside the town of Bethlehem in the Judean wilderness. Imagine brown, not green; think arid and dusty, not lush and damp.

Wherever you read *wilderness* in Scripture, imagine a desert landscape. Directly to the west of Bethlehem is a ridge referred to as Beit Jala. You can find it on a map. This ridge marvelously inclines almost three thousand feet. The paths of this ridge were most likely where the shepherds from Luke 2 were traversing day and night in search of just enough food and water.

SHEPHERDS HERE, THERE, AND EVERYWHERE

In the Old Testament, shepherds were frequent characters and sometimes the most respected. Consider that Abraham was a shepherd; Jacob was a shepherd; Moses was a shepherd; David was a shepherd. Shepherding in the Old Testament required a man to live sacrificially for the sheep. After constructing a makeshift circular pen, shepherds would often sleep in the opening to protect the sheep from wolves in the night. When Jesus said that he is the "gate" (John 10:9), the original hearer would most likely have imagined a shepherd sleeping in the opening. Jesus, therefore, was saying that he is the Good Shepherd, who permits sheep to come in while keeping danger out.

In the Old Testament, shepherd imagery is used as a metaphor for leadership. God leads like a shepherd (see Psalm 23). In the books of the prophets, the coming Messiah was one like a shepherd (see Isaiah 40:11; Jeremiah 31:10). The vocation of shepherding is symbolized as a model for what good leadership looks like: one who provides for and protects the flock.

SHEPHERDING SHIFT

Words, metaphors, and symbols can be tricky. Over the course of time, meanings can change. A symbol or word that meant one thing for a particular generation can come to mean something very different for the next. For example, as an Anglican priest, I sometimes wear a collar in public. From what I have read and experienced, more people are suspicious of clergy than in generations past. On occasion, I receive a harsh word from a stranger, or squinty eyes likely fueled by past wounds. These are always opportunities for me to offer mercy and compassion to those who have been hurt by clergy.

According to the Talmud, shepherds were less respected in first-century Israel than in the Old Testament period. In other words, the shepherding vocation experienced a mood shift in public opinion. Consider that around four hundred years had passed between the writings of the last prophet (Malachi) and the birth of Christ. A lot can change in four hundred years! Therefore, when Luke wrote that shepherds were among the first to lay eyes on the promised Messiah, it was likely a surprise to the original hearer, given the mood shift that had transpired.

In the first century, rather than being regarded as respectable, shepherds were looked at with suspicion. This shift matters significantly when we read about shepherds as among the first to witness the long-expected Messiah. No historian would have written shepherds into the story unless, of course, the story was true. If one were writing fiction, to include shepherds in the narrative would not advance the case that the Messiah was born. Perhaps you're wondering why including these shepherd guys in Luke's gospel would have been controversial. Let me explain.

By the first century, three perceptions of shepherds prevailed:

Shepherds were poor.
Shepherds were rough.
Shepherds were thieves.[1]

Shepherds were almost certainly poor. That was nothing new, as they were poor in Old Testament times too. But grasping the extent of their poverty helps us better understand the other two perceptions. The owners of sheep commonly hired out the difficult job to young boys. In certain seasons, those young shepherds were on the go day after day, night after night, walking the land in search of scarce grass and water. Remember, think sprigs in the wilderness, not alfalfa. That reality meant shepherds kept their flocks continuously on the move. Searching for food and water was a matter of survival. Shepherding was not a desk job; it was dirty, tiresome, smelly work.

The shepherding vocation was also a rough job, best suited for young men. The shepherds of Bethlehem who led their flocks to pasture in places like the Judean wilderness developed rough skin due to harsh weather conditions and being exposed daily to the fierce rays of the desert sun. And their hygiene was often, shall we say, lacking.

I chuckle a bit at Christmas pageants that characterize Luke's shepherds as old men with smooth skin, sweetly whistling "O Little Town of Bethlehem" on a set resembling the English countryside. If that's the image you hold, it's time to shake the Etch A Sketch and redraw a more accurate image.

Another dynamic to consider about shepherds in the story concerns religious life. Shepherds typically worked seven days a week, walking day after day in search of scarce food and water. This meant they could not keep the Sabbath, as required by the law. That was no small deal in the Jewish community. Yet consider how odd it was that they were among the first invited to meet the Messiah! What a strange group of guys to invite to the party. The only way to account for such absurdity is that Luke is writing a factual account.

Unlike the times of the Old Testament, when being a shepherd carried honor and dignity, by the first century, shepherding was not even close to being an aspiring vocation for Jewish boys. Rabbis around the time of Jesus compiled a list of cheating and thieving professions. According to the scholarship of German theologian Joachim Jeremias, shepherds (also referred to as herdsmen) always made the list! As the Roman occupation grew in Palestine, so did the privatization of landownership, offering land that was once public and sometimes private to retired soldiers as payment for years of service.[2] Because the shepherds kept sheep on the move in search of food and water, a shepherd would inevitably herd his flock to graze on privately owned land. One can only imagine the conflict that ensued, in a region of scarce resources, between shepherd and landowner. Just or unjust, shepherds in the first century were perceived to be dishonest thieves stealing the natural resources off others' land. That makes their appearance before the Christ child that much more staggering. New lenses provide us with new insight.

CONTROVERSIAL, NOT CUTE

Shepherding at the time of Jesus was a vocation undertaken only after all other options were exhausted. Why would God choose these guys to be among the first witnesses? It is staggering to consider that these were not likely honest boys who were religiously committed to the coming of the Messiah. Shepherds at that time were not remotely close to being the guys the Jewish world would expect to receive the inaugural invitation to see the Messiah. Luke hinted that the shepherds themselves were shocked at their invitation in the Nativity story, which explains their response:

> An angel of the Lord appeared to them, and the glory of the Lord shone around them, and they were *terrified*. (Luke 2:9)

Why were they terrified? Yes, seeing an angel would probably be so otherworldly that terror would suit the experience. But even more, they had no reason to expect that this holy invitation would be given to *them*. After all, they were just poor, dirty, thieving, non-Sabbath-observing shepherds. Even their own people disrespected them. Why would anyone—especially God—invite them to anything? Even more, why would God's holy angels invite them to be the first guests to worship the Messiah? Oh, mystery of mysteries! A God who loves to turn the tables on the values of this world, inviting those least expected to be the honored guests!

Further in the story, the text reads, "This will be a sign to you: You will find a baby wrapped in cloths and lying in a manger" (verse 12). Why would a baby in cloths lying in a manger be a sign? Is it possible that something more than what is obvious was at work? I suggest the shepherds knew the implications of a baby in an animal-feeding trough. It meant they would find the Christ child amid poverty. It meant that, like the shepherds, he, too, would be poor and dirty. Deeper still, his poverty would be a sign of his identity. Why would *that* be a sign? I suspect the response from the shepherds must have been something like, "A *manger* for the Messiah? That's poor. The Messiah has come like one of us!"

The prophets were telling the truth: The Messiah would be like a shepherd. You can imagine that the good news of the birth of this child did in fact (and still does) cause "great joy" (verse 10) among the lowest of the low. Why? Because God arrived on earth in the socioeconomic bracket of poverty. No one could make this story up.

THE APPROACHABLE CHRIST

The great nineteenth-century English preacher Charles Spurgeon said it well: "We might tremble to approach a throne, but we cannot fear to approach a manger. . . . Never could there be a being more approachable than Christ."[3] The first to witness the Incarnation were shepherds. After Jesus's death, the first to witness his resurrected body were women. No one would expect that, so it must be true. The beginning and end of the Gospels are wrapped in paradox.

It does lead us to wonder, though, *What about the sheep the shepherds left behind when they went to find the Christ child?* Jesus would later say that God's pursuit of us is so relentless and risky that God would leave the ninety-nine sheep to find the lost one (see Matthew 18:12–14). Note that the shepherds also left the ninety-nine to find the One—only the one they found wasn't lost. That child was the one who had come to do all the finding. In other words, the shepherds found the one who had come to find them. In a great reversal, the shepherds became the sheep, and they gathered around a manger that held the one who would become the Good Shepherd of their souls—the one who would become for them the Bread of Life.

No matter your past, God has chosen you. No matter your mistakes, God has chosen you. No matter your social standing, income bracket, or family history, God has chosen you. The invitation to the lowly shepherds reveals the extent to which God has called the least, the last, and the left-outs. Jesus came to find us all. Have you found the One who came to find you?

A FINAL THOUGHT

Over the centuries, many scholars have wondered about the historic significance of Migdal Eder, a specific location outside Bethlehem for breeding lambs. It has been said that the lambs there were raised specifically for the Passover festivals as lambs without blemish. At that location, the lambs were raised and then sold to the temple. During Passover week, the Jewish people would purchase a perfect Migdal Eder lamb at the temple, and on Passover evening, the lamb would be slaughtered to cleanse them from sin and make them remember their flight from Egypt.

If Migdal Eder, outside Bethlehem, is, in fact, where many Passover lambs were raised, it leaves us much to ponder. I cannot help but wonder if those shepherds on that starry night were the same as those tasked to steward the blameless sheep that would be raised for the Passover. How deeply meaningful it would be if they left those sheep only to find the one who would truly become the spotless Lamb who would take away the sin of the world (again, see John 1:29). You cannot make this stuff up. It's not a fable; the story is true.

Reflection

Meditate on Luke 2:8–18, and then reflect on the sketch below. Consider your own story. In what ways have you felt like an outsider? How does God's invitation to the shepherds speak into your personal faith journey?

9

MAGI: GENEROSITY

The Practice of Sacrificial Giving
Matthew 2:1–12

MORE THAN ANY OTHER SEASON, CHRISTMAS IS A time of lavish gift giving. But this task, generous as it is, can be tricky. At least it is for me. I am a terrible gift giver. And Elaina, my wife, can attest to that since she has borne the brunt of some disappointing birthdays and Christmas mornings. In the world of love languages, I am more of a "words of affirmation" kind of guy.[1] Which I guess makes sense, given my vocation. But, to my credit, this is a growth area for me that has improved in some small measure over the years. Elaina, though, may beg to differ.

Imagine you are one of the Magi in the Christmas story. We have no idea how many of them traveled to see Jesus. There could have been three or even thirty-three of these guys. The assumption of "three wise men" is offered because of the three gifts (frankincense, gold, and myrrh). Nevertheless, among the supplies packed for your journey, gifts are in tote for whoever awaits you at the end of that star trail. But have you paused to consider what gifts would befit the King of kings, who already owns "the cattle on a thousand hills" (Psalm 50:10)? Why the gift of gold? What is myrrh, anyway? And as for frankincense, I admit that prior to exposure to the world of essential oils, I'd never laid eyes on the stuff.

Some degree of creativity on the part of the gift giver is necessary for a gift to be experienced meaningfully by its recipient. Like the time Kanye West gave ten Burger King restaurants to his then spouse Kim Kardashian. Or when *Friends* star Courteney Cox gave Jennifer Aniston a twelve-thousand-dollar Chanel bicycle. I'll bet that bike smelled amazing! Or that time when Angelina Jolie gave her then spouse Brad Pitt an actual waterfall. Or when actress Scarlett Johansson presented her then spouse Ryan Reynolds with a necklace featuring one of her wisdom teeth dipped in gold.[2] That's gross. As I said, gifts are tricky.

This book holds the conviction that every detail in the

Scriptures is intentional. What, then, is the Scripture advancing by including the Magi?

1. The Magi have gifts for God.
2. God has gifts for the Magi.

SCRIPTURAL OBSERVATIONS

Turning to the gospel of Matthew for a moment, we read,

> After Jesus was born in Bethlehem in Judea, during the time of King Herod, Magi from the east came to Jerusalem. (2:1)

For the sake of clarity, who exactly are these Magi from the east, and from where did they come? Much ink has been spilt speculating on their precise vocation and origins, but no one knows with certainty. What we do know is that *magi* is the plural form of the singular *magus*. That term could mean "those who possessed superior knowledge and ability, including astrologers . . . and soothsayers."[3] What is worth noting is that the Jewish worldview held magi not only as non-Jewish (therefore Gentiles) but also as sorcerers. Jewish practice at that time was that sorcerers could be stoned to death if caught in the company of Israelites (Exodus 22:18; Deuteronomy 13:10).[4] Later, in the third century A.D., Origen of Alexandria, a Christian theologian, believed "magi are in communion with demons."[5] Suffice to say, the journey of the Magi to see Jesus was a life-threatening pilgrimage in every way.

So, what do we have here? We have a stunning and overtly controversial plot from the opening chapters of Matthew's gospel! Matthew, a Jew, included Gentiles within God's good-news story. And not just run-of-the-mill Gentiles, but foreign stargazers. Even more, pagan sorcerers in search of truth, wherever it leads. We must never reduce the cosmic reach of God's missional heart in this divided world. Surely, that is a primary reason the Magi's treacherous journey toward Christ is included in the Scriptures.

If the Magi were believed to gain insight through demonic powers (reminiscent of ancient Egyptian magicians in the book of Exodus), their story was also about God subverting demonic powers to shine light on the truth. God rescued these pagan sorcerers from their own ignorance and satanic deception. He then used their knowledge of charting stars to guide them toward the location of the one who created the cosmos in the first place (see John 1:1). Remarkable. In the end, the Magi worshipped Jesus, not Satan. As in the story of Joseph traded into Egypt, what was once meant for evil, God used for good (see Genesis 50:20).

CAREER CLIMAX

To my knowledge, every sport has its own version of a draft. A draft is when a team can pick from a pool of new eligible players. In any given sport, players spend years preparing for the moment. Blood, sweat, and tears go into readying oneself for it. I imagine that finally hearing one's name announced and walking toward a stage is enough to move the athlete to weeping and dancing.

Transfer that idea onto the Magi. This was the climax of their careers. For years (perhaps decades), these astrological geniuses had dedicated their lives to charting the stars. These were scientists who saw no need to separate astrology from theology. Perhaps they have much to teach the realm of science today. But where were they from? In her book *Reading the Bible with Rabbi Jesus,* Lois Tverberg wondered,

> Over the ages, Christian readers saw that Matthew's account echoed Psalm 72:10, which pictures kings from Tarshish, Sheba, and Seba paying tribute to the future messiah. They inferred that the visitors were actually royalty from each of these three countries.[6]

What we can say for certain is that, like the athlete's hearing their name in the draft, the Magi's seeing the star soaring in the east would be a cause for weeping and dancing. Imagine all the hard work, the study, the late nights—after all, that is when the stars are visible. Perhaps after napping during the day, they went to work at night. Imagine the haters and doubters of their craft. But in that season, everything they'd spent their life anticipating was arriving. Their shining moment had come, and it was now time to move from speculation in their heads to realization in their feet. Loading the camels, charting the route, packing the gifts—a long and dangerous journey was about to begin.

Off they went in search of the one who had come in search of them. Again, you can't make this stuff up.

ANCIENT PROPHECY

In the ancient Near East, it was customary to bring gifts when a new king was born, and those gifts would represent various goods from the gift giver's place of origin.

Although this theory is often contested, many scholars believe the origin of the Magi to be Arabia, given the extent of the men's wealth, the spices they brought, and the fact that gold at the time was mined from the Arabian region. According to scholar Kenneth Bailey, "Frankincense is a unique product of southern Arabia."[7] Matthew tells us the Magi came "from the east" (2:1), which may simply mean, from a Jewish point of view, east of the Jordan River. That would certainly include Arabia. Whatever the case may be, what is not debated is that the Magi were Gentiles.

But there is still some confusion to clear up about the geography. The Magi came from the east because a star "from the east" appeared in the sky. That's confusing. If they were from the east and saw a star in the east, then you might wonder why they headed west to Jerusalem. I mean, we don't think the Magi circumnavigated the earth to arrive at Jerusalem, do we? No, we don't. They did, in fact, head west to Jerusalem.

So, how do we reconcile this scriptural contradiction? More often than not, contradictions in the Bible are not actually contradictions at all. Displaced from original context, language, culture, and time, it is we who are often the ones who misread the Scriptures. In Hebrew, the word for "east" also means "the rising."[8] So, depending on the Bible translation you are using, the one that reads best is that Magi from the east "saw his star at its rising."[9]

Remember, the Magi were not astrologically shooting from the hip. As learned scientists, they were familiar with sacred texts across traditions. It is reasonable to assume that, because of their access to the Jews through the various exiles over the centuries, they were aware of the Hebrew Scriptures and were perhaps even students of them. Centuries before Matthew, the prophet Isaiah gave us clues about the Magi inclusion in God's global story. In the passage that follows, notice the ancient words in italics. Matthew made an obvious connection between Isaiah's prophecy and the Magi's journey:

> *Arise, shine, for your light has come,*
>   and the glory of the LORD *rises upon you.*
> See, darkness covers the earth
>   and thick darkness is over the peoples,
> but the LORD rises upon you
>   and his glory appears over you.
> *Nations will come to your light,*
>   *and kings to the brightness of your dawn.*
>
> *Lift up your eyes* and look about you:
>   All assemble and come to you;
> your sons come from afar. . . .

> *The wealth on the seas will be brought to you,*
>> *to you the riches of the nations will come.*
> Herds of camels will cover your land,
>> young camels of *Midian* and *Ephah*.
> And all from *Sheba* will come,
>> *bearing gold and incense*
>> *and proclaiming the praise of the* L ORD.
>>> (Isaiah 60:1–6)

The star of light illumined the way for the Magi in search of the one who was to be the Light of the World. The Magi embodied the nations and were as royal dignitaries representing the kings and queens from their homeland. Camels were known as the ships of the desert, given they alone were able to carry the loads of people across the vast Arabian Desert because their peculiar anatomy allowed them to hold water. Kenneth Bailey noted that "Midian and Ephah are tribal lands in northern Arabia, and Sheba was the name for the part of southern Arabia from which the Queen of Sheba came with 'much gold' (1 Kings 10:2)."[10] The reader is meant to connect the dots here that Isaiah's ancient prophecy was fulfilled at the birth of Jesus.

The prophet Micah also spoke of where the future Messiah would be born:

> You, *Bethlehem* Ephrathah,
>> though you are small among the clans of Judah,
> out of you will come for me
>> one who will be ruler over Israel,

whose origins are from of old,
>   from ancient times.
>   (Micah 5:2)

We know the Magi journeyed to Jerusalem. And why wouldn't they? One would think that the King of the Jews would be born in the center of the city. It was at Herod's quarters in Jerusalem (or perhaps his favorite palace many miles south from Jerusalem called Herodium) that the Magi encountered King Herod. They imagined Jerusalem to be the star's pinpoint. So, when the Magi consulted Herod as to the child's whereabouts, he—apparently ignorant about Micah's prophecy—then quizzed the chief priests (Saddu-cees) and teachers of the law (scribes) about the matter. After learning of Micah's prophecy, Herod sent the Magi on their way to find him in Bethlehem, requesting them to alert him when the one they sought was discovered.

Pause for a moment and notice that the Magi quickly gained access to Herod. King Herod was a big deal. His power preceded him. Not only was Herod the greatest builder of that age (and perhaps any age), but also he had put to death all his political rivals, including family members. For a comparison, imagine being part of a foreign dignitary entourage paying a surprise visit (and getting access) to the U.S. president at the White House, or the British prime minister at 10 Downing Street. That tells us the Magi were respected outsiders who likely possessed great wealth and authority.

ADORE, NOT ADMIRE

The Magi uttered a disturbing question to Herod, which most certainly prompted within him a deep insecurity, being the fearful tyrant he was:

> Where is the one who has been born king of the Jews? We saw his star when it rose and have come to worship him. (Matthew 2:2)

History was turning a page, and a significant one at that. In Christ's birth, the new creation was beginning, announced cosmically by a spectacular light rising amid the darkness. John's gospel says that the darkness would conspire against that light but not overcome him (see John 1:5). The star rose, and the Magi journeyed far and wide. The posture of these foreigners when they reached their destination was not to merely admire but to adore! Don't miss that. Upon seeing the baby, they worshipped (Greek: *proskuneo*)!

One of the greatest lies (and clichés) that periodically finds its way back into various churches is that Jesus was a mere human who tapped into a guru-type spirituality. In this paradigm, Jesus was reduced to deserving admiration but certainly not our adoration. This lie, originating in Arian circles since the third century, aimed to dismantle the claim that Jesus was not uniquely fully God and fully man but rather merely human. The Magi didn't fall for this argument. Instead, they fell to their knees, which was the appropriate response before the King of kings and Lord of lords (see Isaiah 45:14; Romans 14:11; Philippians 2:10–11). Wasn't that precisely what took place at the end of John's gospel when the soldiers fell to the ground upon realizing the identity of Jesus (see 18:6)?

Admiration inspires us, but adoration changes us. The Magi saw something unique and cosmic in the Christ child and, thus, fell to their knees, adored with their hearts, and opened their coffers. The moment for gift giving began.

These scientists immediately recognized the infinite worth of the child before them. The one they traveled to meet was no mere infant. This King in the manger possessed a kind of quality that deserved worship and adoration, not just respect and admiration. The prophecies from long ago foretold that a ruler would come. Jesus was (and is) unique, unrivaled, and eternal. And the leadership of Jerusalem, the very people you'd think would be the first to line up and worship him, did just the opposite. Matthew tells us that "all Jerusalem" (meaning Herod, the priests, and the teachers of the law) were "disturbed" by the news (Matthew 2:3). Isn't that how religion often works? Leaders exploit positions to gain power and privilege. They are then threatened by anything or anyone that might question their authority or rival their position. That leads to subtle and not-so-subtle forms of control and manipulation. Herod might be the tyrannical extreme, but, tragically, this dynamic occurs today—at lesser levels—in many religious settings.

It would appear that the Magi were not on a quest for mere scientific inquiry. They were journeying in hopes to discover the One the world had been waiting for—namely, the Messiah who would put the world to rights. A Catholic cardinal from Ghana was once asked by a college student, "What is the difference between American [Christians] and African [Christians]?" He replied, "Americans learn about God and get smart. Africans worship God and are changed." The Magi demonstrated at the foot of the manger that adoration lay at the core of their beings when they encountered the Christ child. At the end of Matthew's account, he says the Magi returned to their country by "another route" (verse 12). As Bishop Fulton Sheen once commented, "Of course they did; for no one comes to Christ and goes back the same way he came!"[11]

GIFTS OF RECIPROCITY

The Magi came bearing gifts. One of the unmentioned rules of gift giving in the ancient Near East was that a "failure to give an appropriate gift dishonors the donor and insults the recipient."[12] The Magi, therefore, brought the best of what they and the royal dignitaries who sent them had to offer. The distance of their journey, combined with the opulence of their gifts, suggested the magnitude of their expectation in the king they were seeking. The extravagance of their gifts revealed their discernment of the child's worth. Perhaps there was something embedded in their astrological studies and the star anomaly happening in the sky that showed this wasn't simply another leader from another nation.

What did the Magi bring? We know they brought *frankincense*. But what exactly is frankincense? It's incense from the resin of trees located in the land of Arabia. Frankincense was used in worship ceremonies (see Exodus 30:4–8; Leviticus 24:7).

We also know they brought *gold*. But why was gold offered? They believed the child at the end of the star was a king; gold befits the honor of a royal king!

They also brought a gift of *myrrh*. Myrrh was used for medicinal qualities but also for burial purposes. Could it be that Matthew was foreshadowing the extent God would go to become a gift for us? The frankincense tells us that Jesus is worthy of worship. The myrrh tells us that this king was born to die. As Bishop Robert Barron once preached, "When you come to Christ, break open the very best of yourself and make it a gift for him."[13] That is precisely what the Magi did.

But there is something crucial Matthew embedded in his telling of the story: Gifts were exchanged, not merely given by the Magi. We usually focus on the gifts they gave and omit the gift they received. Something intimate was taking place in the story of the Magi that a superficial reading of the story misses. One of the reasons the Magi brought such extravagant gifts was because they perceived that the child was indeed the gift the world had been waiting for. In the sacramental traditions of the church, whenever communion is received, the community is reminded by the elements symbolizing the body and blood of Christ that these are "The Gifts of God for the People of God."[14]

The one to whom the Magi brought gifts was himself the greatest gift the world has ever known. We come to God with our gifts (time, talents, treasures), but we always leave receiving the gift of divine presence to carry within us everywhere we go.

BIGGER THAN WE THINK

Did you grow up in a tribe that believed itself to be on the only right path in all the world? As a child, I grew up in a denomination within the Protestant Christian tradition that emphasized the certain damnation of all Roman Catholics. In retaliation, my one Roman Catholic friend reverse condemned me as the one in danger. Who was right? At the time, we didn't care very much because there was a basketball game to play in the driveway. Hell could wait.

I've come to discover that neither position is correct. Labels mean very little. It's the heart that matters. Jesus, too, seemed to care very little about categories we create to box others in and keep people out. He was often found eating with the wrong people, talking with the wrong gender, and healing on the wrong day. I wonder if God sorrowfully nods in cosmic dismay when we attempt to impose our self-righteous judgments on people. To the religious leaders in Jesus's time, he once told them, "I know you. I know that you do not have the love of God in your hearts" (John 5:42). That's haunting. The Magi show us that the love of God shatters our human attempts to restrict spiritual access, inviting all who will to come and see. Author Rebecca McLaughlin wrote, "Jesus hadn't come only for the Jewish people. He was worshiped by foreigners from the first."[15] As a Gentile myself, praise God!

Consider the scandal of the motley crew surrounding the Christ child: To the Jewish world, shepherds were "insider outcasts," while the Gentile Magi were "outsider respectables." Neither group was who you'd expect. From the onset, Scripture provides us with a shocking panorama of God's redemptive plan. Make no mistake: All are invited to the kingdom on God's terms. And at the same time, his grace is more expansive than most people think.

The baby in the manger is the Savior of the world. And the socioeconomic spectrum, from the Magi to the shepherds, is evidence that the world is invited. This stunning, inclusive proclamation *is* the story of Christmas. Scholar Ken Bailey wrote, "The child was born for the likes of the shepherds—the poor, the lowly, the rejected. He also came for the rich and the wise who later appear with gold, frankincense, and myrrh."[16] God really does intend to make good on prophecies such as the one that came through the mouth of Isaiah:

> It is too small a thing for you to be my servant
>> to restore the tribes of Jacob
>> and bring back those of Israel I have kept.
> I will also make you a light for the Gentiles,
>> that my salvation may reach to the ends of
>>> the earth.
>>> (Isaiah 49:6)

This news is so good that our neighbors should seek to eavesdrop on the church during the Christmas season. After all, it's good news for them too.

In ancient times, God's redemptive plan was always bigger than many Jews preferred. Today it is the church that sometimes creates these unnecessary blockades. But each year, the Christmas story awakens us to a God who is bigger than we think and a gospel story that is far more gracious than we realize. I am not suggesting we reduce our theology to some over-spiritualized abstraction or cheap grace as German theologian Dietrich Bonhoeffer warned. Never! Rather, I am suggesting we apply the magnitude of Christian theology correctly. It is God's kindness that leads us to repentance, and not the other way around. Immanuel is the zenith of God's kindness. When we apply theology this way, as we see the gospel of Matthew does, we find that there is room enough for everyone, everywhere, to offer adoration, gifts, and wonder at the sight of the manger.

Jesus was "Lord at thy birth,"[17] the one who holds the entire world in his hands. The Magi knew this. Do we?

ONE FINAL THOUGHT

The Magi were on the move. Their spiritual openness led them to risk and adventure, resulting in deeper revelation and abundant joy. Many people today attest to growing up in religious settings where little movement was necessary. You can be sure that when the only spiritual movement we are invited into is instruction to sit, stand, be quiet, and pay attention, boredom will easily set in. But the Magi teach us to move in our faith! The Magi saw the star, grabbed the gifts, saddled the camel, and hit the road. They were willing to live into an active faith. God still speaks, stars shine, and the Spirit prompts. God is always on the move, inviting us to respond in kind. In what way is God calling you to activate your faith and move this Christmas season?

Perhaps you've been sensing a prompt from God to make a vocational shift that requires faith. Or maybe it's a financial risk for the betterment of someone in need. One of the greatest faith moves we can ever carry out is toward relational repair—to forgive a deep hurt. Or maybe it's a geographical move that you have been ignoring in hopes it would pass.

Faith is like a muscle. To build it, you must use it. In other words, neutral goes nowhere. Every inspiring story in Scripture shares one thing in common: faith. And by faith, I do not mean a bunch of concepts and information we know in our heads. I mean trust—active trust that God is on the move and calling us to respond. Faith involves trusting that God will meet us when we step out where we cannot see. That is one of God's greatest gifts to us. Jesus is Immanuel, God with us. We are not alone. God is still with us. What is one step you can make today, this week, or this season to be obedient to his prompt in your life?

Follow the way of the Magi, and what you'll discover is a movement that leads straight toward Jesus, who is always and ever moving toward us.

Reflection

Slowly read and reflect on Matthew 2:1–12, and then reflect for a time of prayer on the sketch below, wondering, God, how are you calling me to give good gifts and receive your greatest gift again this season?

Herod: Darkness

The Practice of Inviting Light
Matthew 2:1–23

IT HAPPENED AGAIN LAST NIGHT. AS ELAINA AND I engaged in conversation with our neighbors, the exchange inevitably went down a familiar path. Lamenting our cultural direction, one neighbor sighed and said, "I just don't know how much darker it can get." I nodded because I sometimes think the same thing. Maybe you do too.

Honestly, the state of society does, in many ways, feel

dark. The political division feels dark. Hostility within families casts shadows. The technological intrusion of screens feels irresistible. The senseless rise of mass shootings is evil. Go ahead: Insert your felt darkness here: _____.

John, a disciple of Jesus, must have felt the darkness two thousand years ago when beginning his gospel. He was writing to real people experiencing real circumstances. The characters in the Bible were no strangers to darkness. We sometimes think the Bible is a timeless book written outside of context—a book that miraculously fell from the sky. Nothing could be further from the truth. From the darkness, John comforted the church, reminding them (and us) that, again, "the light shines in the darkness, and the darkness has not overcome it" (John 1:5).

It's a strange comfort that darkness is nothing new. Through the course of history, it just takes different shapes and contours. But rest assured, John tells us, that light has come—and is also always coming. As you hold whatever darkness you're experiencing, remember that Jesus, the Light of the World, was birthed amid a great darkness. This darkness was named Herod the Great. His neurotic obsession for greatness provoked unimaginable evil and destroyed countless lives, including that of his own wife and children, whom he murdered.

HEROD, KING OF JUDEA

Who was Herod? The opening chapters of Matthew and Luke name him without going into great detail about his life. At the time, they didn't have to, because the world was well acquainted with his wicked résumé. Ruthless, rich, and anxious, he was a paranoid politician. News that the true King of kings was born didn't sit well with Herod, especially since he knew he was nearing the end of his reign. We are told that a genocide ensued in Herod's futile attempt to preserve his reign (see Matthew 2:16). The timing of Jesus's birth was neither an accident nor a coincidence. He was the Light sent into the darkness.

Before continuing to read about Herod's impact on the Christmas story, take a moment to gaze upon the sketch below. Throughout this chapter, we will return to this piece to help explain why Herod's inclusion in the gospel story is so pivotal.

HEROD THE ~~GOOD~~ GREAT

He was never hailed as "Herod the Good." Goodness implies a high degree of interior quality. When something is good, it usually means quality radiates from the inside out. But have you ever considered the difference between goodness and greatness? I think something can be perceived as *great* without actually being *good* at its core. Greatness often implies an exterior quality of significance—something visible to the human eye. For this reason, goodness is deeper than greatness. According to Paul, goodness is a fruit of the Spirit, but greatness is not (see Galatians 5:22–23). We live in a society that admires exterior greatness but can neglect interior goodness. The world seeks greatness, but the kingdom seeks goodness.

I once bit into an apple that was shiny on the outside but rotten to the core. The apple looked great, but it wasn't good. Herod was great, but he wasn't good. Not even close. According to the world's standards of greatness—success, wealth, and fame—Herod was indeed great. And the opening of Luke's gospel occurred under this shadow of Herod's authority. From the start, the coming of Christ into the world was both socially and politically charged. Jesus did not enter neutral territory. The world was dark.

HEROD THE STRADDLER

Think of Herod as a man straddling two worlds: one foot loyal to Rome, with the other feigning loyalty to the Jews. Manipulating both, Herod wielded his tyrannical agenda. Because Rome ruled the Mediterranean world, Herod appeased Caesar Augustus (Octavian) in order to remain in power. Rome then rewarded him with political power to maintain control over the Jews in Palestine. Because of this, Herod was known as a puppet king. Caesar used Herod to placate Jewish Palestine, which enabled a measure of peace for the purpose of trade. Herod, in turn, used Caesar to gain power and amass wealth. It was the perfect political marriage.

Herod awkwardly straddled loyalties to both Caesar and Israel, yet his true allegiance was to neither but rather to himself.

The reason Matthew and Luke inserted Herod into the story was that they both wanted the reader to know that Jesus entered this dark world. The world's leaders were (are) clamoring for power and control and were (are) governing with deception and self-aggrandizement. The first century was a vulnerable world. Most citizens decidedly supported leaders who could protect them from neighboring enemies—leaders who would stimulate economic prosperity and enflame a nationalistic spirit. Herod checked all those boxes. Many of the Jews hated him but endured him nonetheless due to fear and because he sought to accomplish much for their nation. "Better the devil you know than the devil you don't" perhaps captured the mood of many Jews during the reign of Herod.

Lest we sanitize the Christmas pageant on Christmas Eve, we must remember just how ruthless Herod was. Hebrew scholar Kenneth Bailey wrote,

> The birth of Jesus is always . . . retold in soft colors with beautiful music in the background. The slaughter of the innocents is never a part of any church's "Christmas pageant." . . .
>
> Unspeakable brutality characterizes the beginning and end of Jesus' life.[1]

One thing is for certain: Herod was the anti-Advent character in the Christmas narrative. He was the extreme of one who refused to make room for Christ. Herod was the first "anti-Christ" we meet in the Gospels. He won't be the last. Herod's entire existence opposed the coming of God's kingdom because it threatened his own. This still happens today.

HEROD THE ANXIOUS

When worldly power is acquired, anxiety usually accompanies it. Why? Because opponents clamor for the same power. Power gained, defended, and finally lost is in many ways the story of the world. The arrival of Jesus in the form of a baby was the cause of great concern for Herod the anxious.

Return to the sketch and gaze again:

On the lower right is a humble home in the village of Bethlehem. Why would a child born into such poverty be the cause of such anxiety in a man as powerful as Herod the Great? Read on.

HEROD THE DIPLOMAT

Herod was a brilliant diplomat if there ever was one. Although ruthless, tyrannical, and anxious, he was also opportunistic, cunning, and politically shrewd.

Originally allied with Mark Antony, Herod switched allegiances to Octavian (Augustus) around 30 B.C. once he realized that the future of Rome hailed Octavian—and not Antony—as Caesar. He convinced Octavian to permit him to rule over Palestine on behalf of Rome.

This is where stuff gets a little complicated. Let me make it simple:

Politically, Herod was Roman (appointed by Octavian / Caesar Augustus).

Ethnically, he was Arab (born of a Nabataean mother).

Religiously, he was Jewish (raised in a Jewish household).

Culturally, he was Greek (the language he preferred and the architectural style in which he built).

Talk about a guy with divided loyalties. Herod had more flavors than a Hawaiian pizza. (Pineapple, cheese, and tomato sauce is a ridiculous combination.) Nevertheless, Herod used this complexity to his advantage. Depending on who he was talking to, he could leverage whatever background was necessary in order to advance his will.

In the hall of infamy, Herod joins the ranks among the cruelest rulers in human history (think Nero, Mao, Hitler,

Stalin). He married somewhere around ten women in all and had one of them—his favorite, Mariamne—murdered because he questioned her political loyalty. Her death would haunt him the rest of his life. He later had two of his own sons strangled for the same reason. Herod defended his power at all costs. He was ruthless, but he was also anxious. When Matthew recorded that Herod ordered the genocide of all boys two years old and younger (see 2:16), it is a plausible scenario, given the satanic forces that continuously animated his life.

HEROD THE BUILDER

Israel's geographic position was highly strategic for the trade routes along the Mediterranean Sea and a gateway for lands into the East. Herod controlled the routes for copper, balsam, and sought-after spices, thus showering the land of Israel with wealth unimaginable. In turn, Herod renovated cities in Greek fashion. He also built lavish fortresses for protection, palatial mansions for leisure, multiple temples to the gods of Rome for honor, and a spectacular new temple for the Jews. Even Caesar Augustus was impressed with—and jealous of—the scale and wonder of Herod's building projects. Some speculate Herod was the richest person ever to live.

Herod's temple—dwarfing the previous one, built by Solomon—was a massive five football fields wide by three football fields long, sheathed in white marble. The Talmud says, "Whoever has not seen Herod's Temple has not seen a beautiful building in his life."[2] It is no wonder the Jews were conflicted by his presence. Even the rabbis were impressed by what he built for them. Herod was evil as sin but sometimes helpful too.

Building also meant employing. Over a period of more than forty years, Herod hired more than eighteen thousand workers to build the temple. If you were to pray at the Western Wall today, you'd see the same stones Herod used to build. They are known as Herodian stones, some of which are at least ten feet long by ten feet wide. Machines we have today to lift, carry, and mount stone did not exist at that time. His building methods are a wonder over which we still marvel.

I remind you of this to showcase how complicated it must have been for the Jewish people. Yes, Herod was a tyrannical prop for Rome, but he was also rebuilding the Promised Land. I can't help but wonder if it was tempting for some of the Jews to wonder,

Is Herod the Messiah? Maybe? I mean, look at the way he is rebuilding the land, as the prophecies said would happen.

Is Herod the Messiah? Maybe? Perhaps Herod is just waiting for the right time, when he has just enough power. Then he will overthrow the Romans and re-establish the Promised Land as God's chosen one.

Is Herod the Messiah? Maybe? I mean, "Look . . . ! What massive stones! What magnificent buildings!" (Mark 13:1).

Herod was a tyrant for sure, and the Jews hated him, but they also revered him. Even though he taxed the people to the hilt, he grew the economy. He created jobs, increased exports and imports, and elevated Jewish prominence under Roman rule. I repeat, Herod was evil as sin, but he was helpful too.

I could go on . . .

- I could tell you about his favorite palace, *Herodium,* located not far from Jerusalem and Bethlehem. There he had hot tubs, cold tubs, tepid tubs, all on the top of a man-made mountain in the desert. Crazy!
- I could tell you about his desert fortress, *Masada,* where he imported the choicest of food, wines, oil, and spices and could house up to a thousand soldiers for ten years. Which is pretty crazy.
- I could tell you about *Caesaria Maritima,* his trading port, where he built a freshwater pool in his home on the Mediterranean Sea. Crazy!

. . . but you get the point.

Herod was perhaps the greatest builder of all time. He was rich, ruthless, and anxious.

HEROD AND ESAU

With all this history, perhaps you've mentally drifted a bit. Permit me to pull it all together. What I am about to say you likely didn't hear in Sunday school. Go back with me almost two thousand years before Herod to the age of Jacob and Esau. Deep in the heart of Genesis 25, the story of Herod began.

> Question: *Israel* was the name given to what Jewish father?
> Answer: Jacob.

> Question: And who was Jacob's twin brother? (Hint: the one whose heel he grabbed coming out of the womb.)
> Answer: Esau.

> Question: Esau later became the father of what people?
> Answer: Edomites (later known as Idumeans).

Stay with me, because this is all profoundly connected. Prior to the birth of Jacob and Esau, God spoke to their mother, Rebekah, and predicted war between the sons:

> Two nations are in your womb,
>   and two peoples from within you will
>   be separated;
> one people will be stronger than the other,
>   and the older will serve the younger.
>   (verse 23)

Now fast-forward to the time of Herod. From the line of Esau descended Herod (the Edomite). From the line of Jacob descended Jesus (the Judean). In Genesis 25, Jacob and Esau were two nations warring in the same womb. In Luke 1, Herod and Jesus represented these two nations warring in the same world.

It was prophesied about the line of Jacob, "A star will come out of *Jacob;* a scepter will rise out of Israel. . . . *Edom[ites]* will be conquered" (Numbers 24:17–18). Herod came from the line of Esau, the older. Jesus came from the line of Jacob, the younger. Now, why does any of this matter? Theological bomb alert: because the war that began between Jacob and Esau in the womb of Rebekah all those years ago was finally coming to a climactic conclusion in the struggle between the reign of Herod and the birth of Jesus.

Can you see it? From Genesis to Revelation, the Scriptures are all connected, telling a unified redemption story. The story extends, inviting us to join.

BACK TO BETHLEHEM

Let's return to the art that depicts the home at Bethlehem (from the beginning of the chapter). So serene and quiet. So intimate and humble. The Light of the World had finally come to earth and lay in a manger. If you look to the upper-left side of the sketch below, you will notice a peculiar mountain a few miles beyond the house.

This was Herod's favorite palace, Herodium, which incidentally is now thought to be his probable burial location. It contained four seven-story lookout towers, and from the top

of those towers, Herod had a view of Jerusalem in one direction and Bethlehem in another. Imagine Herod on that tower, gazing toward Bethlehem. He's anxious, ruthless, and alone. The sun is setting, and darkness sets in. Contemplating a genocide, Herod fumes over Micah's prophecy:

> You, *Bethlehem* Ephrathah,
>> though you are small among the clans of Judah,
> out of you will come for me
>> one who will be *ruler over Israel,*
> whose origins are from of old,
>> from ancient times.
>>> (Micah 5:2)

The Genesis story is beginning to find its climax in Bethlehem. The new Jacob has arrived, and the old Esau will not prevail. Herod's tragic attempt to annihilate God's plan is futile.

But let's not let ourselves off the hook here. Herod's story is a cautionary tale of a life that slowly but surely got complicated by powers of the world. Herod was the extreme of a life that refused to make room for God. He became enmeshed with the satanic powers that animate the human struggle. We, too, struggle with temptations on one level or another.

We crowd God out of our lives, leaving little room when we entangle ourselves in the lies of

1. *Consumerism:* Consumerism promises identity but leaves us with anxiety. It's the lie that our identity can be purchased—the satanic trap that we never have enough. Like Herod, we seek to buy more and build bigger in the hope of becoming someone important.

2. *Comparison:* Comparison promises dignity but leaves us with anxiety. It's the lie that we are never enough, seducing us to believe we must be greater, prettier, and smarter than others.

3. *Cynicism:* Cynicism promises safety but leaves us with anxiety. It's the lie that we can't ever know enough, so why trust in anything beyond ourselves? Cynicism sacralizes doubt, warning us to never give our hearts away to God.

Herod wrestled with each of these temptations in the extreme. So do we. Christmas is the invitation to make room for the One who has arrived to conquer our temptations. Christ has won the victory and invites us to rest in his story. Will you choose to make room—to enfold your smaller story into the greatness of his?

Reflection

Slowly read Matthew 2:1–23, and then reflect on the sketch below. Ultimately, Herod isn't great. Jesus is. And Jesus, not Herod, is the one the world is still beholding today. Will you, also?

Caesar Augustus: Authority

The Practice of Stewarding Power

Luke 2:1

ANOTHER POLITICIAN EMBEZZLES FUNDS. ANOTHER clergyman abuses children. Another CEO gaslights employees. Another company underpays women. Another misguided teen shoots students. The list goes on and on and on. These are just a few of the tragic misuses of power we have come to know well. Many people today are weary and wary of power.

Power—and the struggle to claim it—has existed since Cain killed Abel. The question of power is not *if* but *how* it is used. Power is experienced differently around the world, depending on who has it and which side of it you're on. Jesus taught that when power is used positively, it looks like someone who offers their resources for the benefit of others (see Matthew 10:42). He also critiqued the misuse of power, illustrating the evil of one who has access to bread and fish but chooses instead to give stones and snakes (see 7:9–10). He taught that God, unlike humankind, is not like that. He never wields power to exploit or withhold. Rather, he gives bread to the hungry and water to the thirsty, and we should become like him and do likewise with whatever power we have.

At the end of Matthew's gospel, Jesus told his disciples that all power and authority (Greek: *exousia*) are his, and he gives it freely to advance his kingdom on earth. The problem with power, therefore, is not that it exists but that it is misused. At the birth of Jesus, the blatant misuse of power through the emperor of Rome, Caesar Augustus, was no exception.

A TALE OF TWO STORMS

It's called the Fujiwhara effect: a rare weather occurrence when two storms of considerable power come within eight hundred miles of each other (or about the length of the state of California). When that happens, the two storms dance.[1] But what happens after they dance is even more fascinating. The larger storm typically absorbs the weaker, growing in power as a result. Like a superstorm, this phenomenon symbolizes the "dance" of the two oppressive leaders running the world when Jesus was born: Caesar Augustus and Herod the Great. Powerful storms they were, dancing about in conquest and opulence as the least, lost, and left-outs mourned and wailed. The two leaders were each deceived to think of themselves as the messianic gift the world was waiting for.

Imagine Herod as the smaller of the two storms, tyrannically hovering over Palestine as a puppet king in service to Rome. Dark, powerful, and generating fear, he caused widespread frustration among the Jews even as he used his political platform to rebuild the nation. However, fierce as Herod was, there was an even larger storm looming: a storm called Augustus, whose mission was to absorb the world into his sphere of authority. The two leaders together were like a Fujiwhara effect. The emperor of Rome was given the name Octavian at birth. He later changed it to Caesar Augustus ("exalted one"). Beyond a doubt, Octavian was the most powerful of all the Caesars.

According to Paul, the timing of Jesus's birth was not coincidental (see Galatians 4:4–5). At the proper time, God the Father sent God the Son into a world saturated by evil storm systems. Instead of avoiding the suffering of humankind, Jesus took on flesh and descended to "dance" between the storms, finally absorbing their decreasing power into a cross-shaped tree.

Luke included Caesar in his gospel because he believed the days of Augustus were the perfect time for God's redemptive plan to invade the power structures of the world.

I want to emphasize just how powerful and disturbing was the storm we call Caesar. Just as Babel had, Rome was uniting the world through a universal language, the building of roads, advances of technology, and "franchising" culture. The mission of Augustus was to acquire, consolidate, and distribute his power, arrogantly assuming the role that belongs uniquely to God, Father of all.

According to Luke, it was Augustus's census that sent Joseph and Mary to register at Bethlehem. The purpose of the census was to extract more taxes from an already overtaxed people. Luke didn't intend for us to miss the irony: God used Caesar's unjust census to send the couple to Bethlehem, thus fulfilling the ancient prophecy to unleash justice in the world. The humor and subversion are glaring. God has a history of redeeming evil in the world to bring about his good and perfect plan (see Genesis 50:20, for example).

COMET IN THE SKY

Go back with me to before Augustus was crowned emperor. It was a time when he was just Octavian. Imagine the scene: A stadium called Circus Maximus is jam-packed with zealous Romans.[2] Once a year, this legendary stadium hosts games for seven days to honor the late and great Julius Caesar. The crowd is electric, rising to their feet as the chariots race by. They will later fist the air when the animals duel, and after that they will chant for death at the gladiatorial games.

But this year, something strange lingers in the air— literally!

In 44 B.C., while the games are occurring, a comet lingers in the sky every day around the eleventh hour. Over the course of the week, the question circulates through the crowd: What does the comet mean? Consensus grows that the comet must be the soul of the beloved and deceased Julius Caesar. Julius is finally ascending to his place among the gods, they think. And if that is true, his adopted son, Octavian, must be the son of a god and more worthy of the throne than his current rival, Mark Antony.[3] Later in his reign, Augustus will inscribe the comet onto the coin that bore his image. In the eyes of the people, the comet phenomenon at the games legitimizes the absolute power Augustus will bequeath himself to rule the world.

Consider the titles attributed to Caesar Augustus:

1. *Divine Son of God.* "This, this is he whom thou so oft hearest promised to thee, Augustus Caesar, son of a god, who again set up the Golden Age."[4]

2. *Gospel.* "Since the birthday of the god Augustus was the beginning of the gospel (good news) for the world."[5]

3. *Peace (Pax Romana).* "As long as Caesar is the guardian of the state, neither civil dissension nor violence shall banish peace."[6]

4. *Savior.* "Since Providence, which has ordered all things and is deeply interested in our life, has set in most perfect order by giving us Augustus, whom she filled with virtue that he might benefit humankind,

sending him as a savior both for us and for our
descendants."[7]

5. *Forgiver of Sins*. "Thine age, O Caesar, has brought
   back fertile crops to the fields . . . has wiped away
   our sins and revived the ancient virtues."[8]

Any of these titles sound familiar? Before his death in
A.D. 14, Caesar Augustus wrote an autobiography chronicling the magnificence of his eternal legacy. Subversively,
near the end of the first century, Luke wrote Acts of the
Apostles, the sequel to his gospel, chronicling the magnificence of the Holy Spirit. (Wink, wink.) You think Luke had
a bone to pick with Rome about who really holds all power
and authority? I do! Luke's Acts was a glaring (and controversial) refutation about the fleeting power of any Caesar
written to anyone willing to listen in the Roman world.

Don't miss the plot! Jesus, the Prince of Peace, the Savior
and Divine Son, the forgiver of sins who embodies the good
news (gospel) in himself, was born at a time when Caesar
assumed those titles for himself. The irony was thick. The
dance was on.

STORIES AND STRUCTURES

For decades, Caesar Augustus successfully amassed and
abused power across the world. His successors did the same.
But before the age of twenty-four-hour news coverage and
rampant social media, "how [did] one convince millions of
people to believe particular stories about gods, or nations?"[9]

It's simple, really: through the art of storytelling and architectural structures. Augustus hired poets such as Virgil to create and spread stories that explained "who Caesar was, what Caesar did, and why everyone was so fortunate to be living under his rule and reign."[10] Within Virgil's stories (*Aeneid,* for example) were the embedded Roman morals and values to assimilate conquered nations across the earth. Ever wonder why theaters existed in every ancient city in antiquity? Theaters were dramatizing events not merely for the purpose of entertainment but also for the purpose of indoctrinating and enculturating new people into Rome's message and mission, all through the power of dramatic storytelling.

Augustus also built structures to help everyone feel at home no matter where they traveled in the empire—on the road he built, by the way. For example, every Roman town would have a temple of worship, a bathhouse for leisure, an amphitheater for sport, an agora for shopping, toilets for sanitation, and so forth. Rome wanted to franchise the world.

Once a foreign city was conquered, it was then converted to the superior Roman way of life. The structures served to reinforce how good it was to be a civilized Roman.[11] So when someone traveled for business—for example, from Ephesus (Turkey) to Scythopolis (Palestine), both located in the Roman Empire—they felt at home in a foreign city because of a sense of architectural familiarity providing them leisure, fresh water, and worship to the gods and emperor.

In a reflective moment before his death, Augustus said, "I found a city built of sun-dried brick. I leave her clothed in marble."[12] He wasn't kidding.

Augustus, Son of a God

Jesus was born into a politically charged, power-hungry world. When we read Luke, it is helpful to train our ears to hear his gospel with political sensitivity. For example, Luke announced,

> I bring you *good news* that will cause great joy *for all the people.* Today in the town of David a *Savior* has been born to you; he is the Messiah, the Lord. (2:10–11)

Luke's announcement was deeply political. By *political,* I don't mean partisan. God doesn't kowtow to any human political party. God is God's own politics. The way he arranged the kingdom and sent the Son are the politics of the kingdom. Jesus's Sermon on the Mount was the greatest kingdom stump speech the world ever heard. If you want to know God's politics, read the Gospels. The political approach is why Herod was troubled and why Caesar should have been.

Before Luke's announcement, similar ones were made about Caesar. The early Christians in the Roman world would have known about the divine claim regarding Augustus written in 9 B.C. from the city of Priene (in present-day Turkey). About Octavian's birth, it was heralded,

Providence . . . has set in most perfect order by giving us Augustus, whom she filled with virtue *that he might benefit humankind,* sending him as a *savior* both for us and for our descendants, that he might end war and arrange all things, and since he, Caesar, by his appearance (excelled even our anticipations), surpassing all previous benefactors . . . and since the birthday of the god Augustus was the beginning of the good tidings [*good news*] for the world.[13]

Notice the similarities between Luke's announcement of Jesus and Priene's earlier announcement about Augustus.

1. good news (that is, the gospel)
2. for all people (that is, global)
3. the birth of a savior (that is, salvation)

Luke did not write into a void; he wrote into a context that would have known about the (false) claims of Caesar. From the opening lines, Luke urges his reader (you and me) to make a choice. Is Caesar the Lord or is Jesus? Who is the Savior for the world? Will the real good news please stand up? Did you know that you can visit Augustus's mausoleum in Rome? It's a circular structure along the Tiber River. His ashes may remain there today, resting lifelessly next to the dust. On the other hand, Jesus's remains are nowhere on earth to be found.

If the announcement of Luke is true, God's humor and humility are on full display. We often identify power in the form of wealth, weapons, palaces, and possessions. But on that cold and starry night long ago, the shepherds of Bethlehem would have been shocked to find King Jesus in a humble manger and not a palatial fortress. Power behaving humbly doesn't have much of a history. Humility wasn't even considered a virtue in the Roman world. Humility was a sign of weakness, not strength. Caesar wielded his power to lord over, not serve under. Jesus warned his disciples about this type of leadership (see Matthew 20:25; Mark 10:42). He also said one will recognize the great leaders because with their power they choose to serve (see Matthew 23:11). Kingdom leaders exercise power to advance the flourishing of "the least of these" (25:40) rather than exploit it for self-indulgence.

Some might argue, "But wait. Didn't Caesar install relative peace on earth through the use of his power?" I'm glad you asked.

THE PRINCE OF PEACE

Caesar's program for peace was officially called the Pax Romana (Roman peace), and—to his credit—under his reign, an unprecedented period of worldwide stability occurred throughout much of the Roman world. Virgil announced to the world an eternal age of peace that Caesar's reign had ushered in: "This, this is he whom thou so oft hearest promised to thee, Augustus Caesar, son of a god, who again set up the Golden Age."[14] Wow! A golden age set up by a prince of peace! Wouldn't everyone want to be a part of that? It depends.

Whereas many of the peace efforts to quell wars and suppress violence were mostly effective under Caesar, his methods to achieve this end were seldom noble and never holy. My friend Brad Nelson has taught, "Whether you enjoyed Caesar's 'peace' depended on which end of the sword you found yourself on."[15] Romans wanted you to need them. They seduced foreign leaders and cities with the promise of water, toilets, leisure, entertainment, and boundless bread. But if that wasn't the brand of peace you longed for, Rome would eventually force you to submit by the sword.

Brad Gray, creator of *The Sacred Thread,* asserted that by the time of Caesar Augustus, the Roman army had become a full-time, highly organized, professionally paid army— well over a quarter million strong.[16] That's huge! For context, the city of Jerusalem at that time was home to around eighty thousand inhabitants.[17] Caesar announced peace, but the sword was always nearby if necessary.

What Rome failed to comprehend was that true peace is not merely the absence of violence, physical or otherwise, nor is peace merely access to bread and leisure. True peace is the presence of soul-fulfilling, God-given qualities such as joy, love, purpose, hope, and renewal. True peace always carries with it a sense of agency and liberty for its recipients. No political party can perfectly install that kind of government on earth—not then, and not now. That is why Jesus came to earth. That is why we wait for him to come again. *He* is the Prince of Peace, not Caesar.

PEACE ON EARTH TODAY

In 2016, as a spiritual and political discipline, I gave equal attention to watching the Republican and Democratic conventions. Being an American citizen, I wanted to give both candidates a chance to earn my vote. To my sadness, both candidates woefully overpromised in ways that felt borderline delusional—Caesarean, in fact.

At the conclusion of one convention, a candidate announced, "The terrorism in our cities . . . threaten[s] our very way of life. . . . I alone can fix it."[18] I thought, *Really? You alone?* The speech was a salvation script. Was this person really our only hope? I don't think so.

Weeks later, the other candidate declared, "I'm the last thing standing between you and the apocalypse."[19] I thought—again—*Really? You are the mediator between heaven and earth?* This was a messianic script. That year, I wanted to write in Jesus for president. And, really, every year, if I'm honest. Rome might have fallen, but the Caesarean pursuit of power is still alive today. On this topic, Catholic scholar Michael Patrick Barber was spot-on: "The Gospel writers reveal that hopes for salvation are not to be pegged on political figures. . . . Jesus lost the only election in which he was up for vote; the crowds chose Barabbas instead of Christ."[20] Do we trust Jesus and the peace he seeks to give? The felt arrival of his peace isn't always as immediate as we'd like, but it's full of grace and truth, present now and forevermore.

LARGO DI TORRE ARGENTINA

Largo di Torre Argentina is an ancient square in Rome. Filled with the ruins of temples and a theater, it is believed to be the location where Julius Caesar was murdered. At the time of Jesus, the square was magnificent. Rome, the eternal city, was clothed in marble by Caesar Augustus. His autobiography boasted of great acts (or deeds) to be forever remembered. Through his acts, Augustus believed he could attain an eternal legacy as the dispenser of peace. But today when you walk this square in Rome, it's filled not with legacy but with hundreds of feral cats who daily urinate on its ruins. To gaze upon its desolation is an exercise in pondering the power given to humankind.

Isaiah was right: Human power fades like grass (see 40:8). Even Caesar's power. God's Word alone endures. Isaiah would again prophesy about a child who would come into the fiercest political storm known to earth:

> To us a child is born,
>> to us a son is given,
>> and the government will be on his shoulders.
> And he will be called
>> Wonderful Counselor, Mighty God,
>> Everlasting Father, Prince of Peace.
> Of the greatness of his government and peace
>> there will be no end.
>>> (9:6–7)

As we await today the Second Advent, ours is the blessed vantage point of inserting his name:

> To us *Jesus* is born,
>> to us *Jesus* is given,
>>> and the government will be on *Jesus's* shoulders.
> And *Jesus* will be called
>> Wonderful Counselor, Mighty God,
>> Everlasting Father, Prince of Peace.
> Of the greatness of *Jesus's* government and peace
>> there will be no end.
>>> (adapted from verses 6–7)

Jesus alone can fix this. We may doubt many things, but when Luke inserts Augustus into the beginning of the story, it leaves no room for doubt that Jesus was born into a political storm. Jesus arrived at a war-torn, power-hungry battlefield that is still contested to this day. Christmas is not the telling of a sweet story illustrated best by Precious Moments figurines, nor is it best told through the snowy village decor that nests high atop the kitchen cabinets, dreamy as those are. Christmas is the announcement of peace within a cosmic Fujiwhara effect. Today intrusive storms lurk in several areas of our lives, seeking to absorb us into their chaos. Christmas is the good news that amid the battles waged that burrow all the way to the center of the human heart, there is one who still brings peace where there is none.

At the time of Jesus's birth, Augustus had no idea that

this little baby would grow up to calm the storms in all the earth. One night while on the Sea of Galilee, Jesus's disciples fearfully woke him in the middle of a storm. He arose, extended his hand, and spoke to the chaos: "Quiet! Be still!" (see Matthew 8:23–27). The storm ceased. Our storms, also, will one day cease. Until that time, we trust that the just one, the Divine Son, the Savior of the world and forgiver of sins, will come to restore peace on earth, goodwill to humankind.

Reflection

Slowly read and reflect on Luke 2:1. Then spend some time meditating on the sketch below, wondering, How am I wielding the power God has given me? How am I stewarding power for the good of others? Where am I squandering it to serve only myself?

SIMEON: EXPECTATION

The Practice of Active Waiting

Luke 2:22–35

SIMEON WAS A RIGHTEOUS AND DEVOUT MAN WHO patiently waited for the Messiah's arrival. Prompted by the Holy Spirit, he first encountered Jesus as a baby in the temple courts. Simeon's (very) brief appearance in Luke helps us notice how expectant waiting opens our lives to receiving the fullness of God's gifts. The clearest way to observe spiritual growth is by looking back on our personal journeys.

The Danish philosopher Søren Kierkegaard once said, "Life can only be understood backwards."[1] Now that we are in the Christmas season of lavish receiving, permit this chapter to guide you backward, reflecting on how waiting in Advent secures blessing in Christmas.

GREAT EXPECTATIONS

Expectations matter. Sometimes our expectations disappoint us, leading to sorrow. But sometimes they surprise us, ending in joy.

When I was seven years old, I wanted a telescope, and I wanted one badly. My expectations grew as the days advanced toward Christmas. With the season of receiving gifts upon us, it seemed the perfect time to launch a long vocation in astronomy. After informing my parents of my career plan and imminent need for a magnification device, I created space in my bedroom and awaited its arrival. My new giant telescope would soon fit snugly between the dresser and closet, providing the necessary angle through the window for an evening charting of the cosmos.

The expectation was high . . .

The room was prepared . . .

The time was nigh . . .

The intergalactic epic was about to begin . . .

Until . . . *it didn't.*

To their credit, my parents did, in fact, purchase a telescope for me that Christmas, but they got it from the toy aisle at Walmart. Rather than the giant apparatus expected, the device was about the length and width of a baseball bat. Making matters worse, the viewing power of said device rivaled that of my uncle's mediocre binoculars. Thus, my astronomy career was stifled, never to be pursued again. Selah.

I remember feigning gratitude for that gift on Christmas morning, but the disappointment in my heart was palpable. Had my parents not known that I needed better gear than this? Had they not perceived what was to be the launch of an impressive future for their little boy? Or perhaps they were just trying to stay reasonably within budget. Whatever the case, that December 25, the space between my expectations and reality created a gap. There is a name for that gap. We call it disappointment.

Unmet expectations are disappointing. We expect A but experience B. That's disappointment. We've all been there. This applies across the range of human life from trivialities like crappy telescopes to significant realities like faith. Simeon held firmly to expectations about the kingdom of God advancing in his lifetime. For years, he waited, and for decades, nothing happened. Sound familiar? Those decades of disappointment could have ended in hopelessness and despair, but they didn't. Instead, the waiting fueled Simeon's expectation further and became an example of what it looks like to wait expectantly for the promises of God despite not fully experiencing them on our timelines.

PRESENTATION OF JESUS

Several years ago, a person in my church berated me for months over my conviction to preach and teach Jesus through a Hebrew lens. She said I wasn't American enough for her taste and questioned my loyalty to the nation. Soon after, she left with her family to find another church. Everybody won. I bring it up because one would be hard-pressed to minimize the Jewishness of Mary and Joseph as they made their way to the temple in Jerusalem to dedicate their firstborn son:

> When the time came for the purification rites required by the Law of Moses, Joseph and Mary took him to Jerusalem to present him to the Lord (as it is written in the Law of the Lord, "Every firstborn male is to be consecrated to the Lord"), and to offer a sacrifice in keeping with what is said in the Law of the Lord: "a pair of doves or two young pigeons." (Luke 2:22–24)

There are at least two things happening here. First, Mary sought ceremonial purification—as Jewish women did—at the temple after bleeding in childbirth (see Leviticus 12:1–8). Second, Jesus, as the firstborn son, was presented and then redeemed in order to return home with the family rather than remaining in service at the temple.

Luke mentions an ancient ritual called pidyon haben, which goes all the way back to the Exodus, when Israel fled Egypt. Think of the presentation and redemption like a tithe: The first and best are given to the Lord. When a family had the firstborn son, that child belonged wholly to God, and the parents were to offer the baby to remain at the temple for service. Remember in the Exodus from Egypt when God spared from death the firstborn sons of Israel? This ritual recalls that. Later, an instruction was given that the descendants of Aaron (that is, Levites), not the firstborn sons of all Israel, would become the priests. Therefore, the ritual of pidyon haben required parents to offer a small gift to the priests in order to "redeem" their firstborn son from the priesthood and take him home with them to live.[2] Everybody won.

Verses 6–8 state that a lamb was required for Mary's purification but that if a couple was poor, as most Jews were at that time, a pair of doves or pigeons could be used for sacrifice instead. Luke tells us that the couple offered the latter, which is to say, they were poor. Jesus, eternal Creator and King of kings, was born into poverty.

Why does any of this matter? Expectations.

There are at least two things we can conclude from this.

1. Expectations Are Good

But . . . when our expectations are built upon assumptions based on personal preferences rather than humble surrender, they often lead to disappointment and despair when things don't turn out the way we want. I've been there. Maybe you have too.

These real disappointments often go something like this:

*I thought God was calling me to move, but now I wonder
    if I misheard, because life is hard.
I thought God would heal, but that healing never came.
I thought God would restore the relationship, but nothing
    ever seems to change with that person.*

> *I thought God would provide, so why am I struggling to find a job?*
>
> *I thought God would guide, but why have my kids wandered so far?*

Each of these disappointments share a common root: *I thought God . . .* First, it is possible that you *did* hear God. It's just that what you heard sometimes looks and feels different from how you imagined it would. Sometimes we hear God perfectly and respond in obedience and things still don't unfold the way we thought they would. That happens all the time. You are not alone. I wonder if Simeon was at first a bit surprised to sense the Spirit confirm the Messiah's identity through a poor, ordinary couple.

2. Expectations Are (Again) Good

God doesn't work on *our* timelines. And let's face it: They demand immediacy. That is what makes Jesus's timeline to raise Lazarus so puzzling (see John 11:6). Like many people in Israel, Simeon probably assumed that the liberation of Israel was immediate and political. I wouldn't blame him, given the prophecies that were central in Jerusalem.

In some ways, his expectations were right. Jesus had come to personally liberate the world from sin and death. But the liberation Israel was waiting for would take time to unfold. God is far more patient than we are comfortable with. Perhaps the very reason he gives us time is so not everything has to happen at once. There may be some things we are hoping for right now and not seeing results for, but sometimes God works slowly over generations to fulfill promises.

In your reflections this Christmas season, create some space to wonder in your heart,

> *Am I in it for the long haul with God?*
> *Am I willing to wait on the promises?*

The way you answer those questions will determine whether your spirituality is better characterized as *relational* or *transactional*. Relational faith says, "God, *with* you I want intimacy." Transactional faith says, "God, *from* you I want immediacy." Relational faith is willing to wait actively, growing in devotion and focus. Transactional faith waits passively, drifting slowly away into a sea of distraction and apathy. Relational faith says, "I trust you, Lord, and am willing to wait on your redemptive action." Transactional faith says, "Do this now, God, or I will seek help elsewhere."

This thread is continuously woven through the Scriptures. Hear these convicting words from the book of Hebrews:

> These [God followers from the Old Testament] were all commended for their faith, yet none of them received what had been promised, since God had planned something better for us so that only together with us would they be made perfect. (11:39–40)

Here's the thing: When we suffer disappointments, most of us don't want to hear from the Bible. I get it, and I don't blame you. But if you think the Bible is a collection of stories about other people who experienced only wild success and immediate answers, then read again. It's mostly a collection of stories about other people who chose to hold on to faith despite *not* receiving everything they had hoped for in this life.

Be encouraged. If you find yourself in a season of disappointment, take heart. Remember that there is the cloud of witnesses who can empathize and are waiting—with you—for the fulfillment of all that is to come. Revelation, the final book of the Scriptures, ends with a plea for Jesus to come soon. The implication of this is that we are still waiting for the full arrival of God's kingdom.

SIMEON THE BLESSED

Simeon counted himself blessed to have merely laid eyes on the Christ. He was now ready to depart this life, even though he knew there was more to come. Simeon realized that his own small story was connected to a larger story that God would unfold slowly over millennia. Likewise, God has invited us to join that same long story that is slowly unfolding. We are each a very small but significant part of that story.

Whatever shattered expectations you presently sit with, know that the story—your story, our story, God's story—is not finished. His redemptive plan will have the final word in every matter under the sun. Whether in your closest relationships, your singleness, your children, your job, your wounds, or your failures, all tears will one day be forever wiped away, swallowed up in a joy everlasting that makes all things new. Everybody wins!

So, over a sustained period of time, Simeon practiced a very hard discipline. He waited. But notice he wasn't alone in the waiting:

> There was a man in Jerusalem called Simeon, who was righteous and devout. He was *waiting for the consolation of Israel,* and the Holy Spirit was on him. (Luke 2:25)

Here was a man of longing, hope, and vigilance. Israel was a nation burdened, weary, and lamenting their oppression from Rome. They waited for the Messiah. I imagine some waited with hope while others waited in despair. That is important to notice here. Some were willing to wait in a way that grew their faith in God, while others shrank in faith because of waiting.

Not to be flippant, but I live in South Carolina and observe firsthand how this plays out in college football. I have never seen a college football fan base as hopeful as the South Carolina Gamecocks'. I've personally witnessed these fans as some of the most resilient to consistent disappointment. Truly, they can patiently wait with great hope on a team that cannot seem to get it together. Days turn into years, and years turn into decades. It's remarkable—their hope, that is.

I'm not trying to compare faith to football, but it is important for Christians today to remember we are still waiting for Jesus to return to earth. We still await the day when all shall be well, when all tears are wiped away forever, and when the sun shall never set again because of the radiance of Christ's light.

We are all, in various areas of our lives, waiting. The question isn't about *if* we wait; rather, it's about *how* we wait. One form of waiting leads to cynicism, while another leads to hope. I wonder where you tend to find yourself on that continuum. Ours is a culture of immediacy, and waiting is hard.

ACTIVE WAITING

In the first century, the people of Israel found themselves— once again—needing God to come to their rescue. "Hosanna!" Who could blame them? Psalm 94 is the perfect song to sum up the mood of that time. "How long, LORD?" (verse 3). We have all prayed a form of that psalm, some more recently than others.

Simeon was an aged man in Luke's gospel. His waiting had persisted for decades. But the Holy Spirit was on this man, and we cannot discount the impact the Spirit has on us in our surrendered waiting. The Spirit had slowly formed Simeon over time into a "righteous and devout" man (Luke 2:25). Like stones that have become smooth from water running over them, Simeon had been well formed in the waiting. Although his years had accrued, his expectation that the Messiah would come had not diminished.

Simeon is a model of what Advent is meant to produce in us as we anticipate Christmas morning. The season of Advent prepares us to receive what our hearts truly long for, and that monthlong period of waiting shapes us. As the ancients awaited the first coming of Christ, so we now await the second coming. The church today needs new Simeons: people becoming more righteous and devout amid waiting, which is to say that gap between expectation and reality.

But we hate to wait. Our lives conspire toward immediacy. From grocery lines to traffic lights, from the doctor's office to bingeing shows, waiting has become torturous—unacceptable, even. One of the cellphone's functional purposes now is to distract us while we wait. But maybe Simeon has something to teach us about our own waiting. Maybe he models for us *how* to wait in a more meaningful, purposeful way. Maybe he invites us to consider waiting as an opportunity and not a problem. Consider this the next time you're stuck in traffic.

Waiting can be *active,* or it can be *passive.* This makes all the difference when one wants to sustain expectation over the long haul. Looking at the cellphone while waiting in line is an example of passive waiting. We wait frustratingly, seeking distractions to keep us busy and entertained. In the following chart, consider how we respond to waiting:

	Active Waiting	**Passive Waiting**
hearts	enduring faithfulness	impatient entitlement
minds	growing imagination	wandering boredom
wills	sustained focus	cynical resignation

As Simeon waited, he grew in righteousness and faithfulness to God's people and plan. Luke called him "devout" (verse 25). We derive *devotion* from this word. Simeon did not passively wait for the plan of God to arrive, busying himself in aimless distraction. In passive waiting, our hearts grow cold and wander, our minds grow dull and seek amusement, and our wills become cynical and resigned.

But Luke tells us that Simeon waited actively for God's plan to unfold. Waiting can grow our faith commitment or shrink it. For Simeon, waiting for the Messiah grew his faith until the fullness of time had come. Even in Simeon's old age, his heart warmed in anticipation of the arrival of the Messiah. Active waiting causes us to remain centered on that which we seek rather than reaching for substitutes that do not satisfy. Active waiting also deepens our mental capacity to become patient as we anticipate what we most desire.

Cynicism runs rampant today. But God wants to raise up a new generation willing to actively wait, expectant that Jesus will again come. In the meantime, we are called to grow in righteousness, arranging our lives according to the ways of the coming kingdom.

When we actively wait, our minds remain steadfast, enduring the gap between expectation and reception. As we wait, we are called to battle against the mood of cynicism, immediacy, and entitlement. When we actively wait, our hearts remain emotionally loyal and not fickle like the Israelites when Moses tarried with God on the mountain. When we actively wait, our lives remain engaged in the present moment, focused on engaging acts of kindness and justice, even when we feel stuck or sense that God is distant.

WAITING AND THE HOLY SPIRIT

It is important to notice that the Holy Spirit was on Simeon. That day of his encounter at the temple, Simeon didn't analyze his way to Jesus. One of the gifts of active waiting is the filling of the Spirit into the empty space of our lives. When Joseph and Mary brought Jesus into the temple for dedication, it was the Spirit who opened Simeon's eyes to the messianic identity of the child. Later, after Peter confessed Jesus's messianic identity, Jesus told him, "This was not revealed to you by flesh and blood, but by my Father in heaven" (Matthew 16:17). Likewise, the Spirit revealed to Simeon the identity of the child and also the fate of Mary (see Luke 2:25–35).

Simeon's entire life culminated at that moment in the temple. Afterward, he was ready to depart and be with the Lord (see verse 29). He became one of the first witnesses to see the salvation promised for the world and proclaimed that the child was not merely a prophet or rabbi but salvation incarnate (see verse 30).

Everybody wins!

Reflection

Slowly read Luke 2:22–35, and then reflect on the sketch below. Consider what active waiting practically entails in a specific gap you are facing between expectation and fulfillment.

13

ANNA: SCRIPTURE

The Practice of Prophetic Imagination

Luke 2:36–38

I WASN'T RAISED IN A FAITH COMMUNITY THAT PUR-
sued dynamic experiences with God. But from a young age,
I felt in my soul a longing for a faith that was deeper than
mere head knowledge. Although many people told me God
no longer does miraculous acts since we now have the Bible,
I've long believed it presumptuous to tell him what is and is
not possible.

I remember a specific moment in my late twenties when I made a choice to follow the Spirit, wherever God might lead, even beyond my comfort zone. Years later, that choice led me to a conference where I'd heard that God was moving in ways that were definitely beyond that zone of comfort. To up the ante (and add credibility), I invited two of my staff (neither of which came from a charismatic-religion background) to join me.

We found the first day of the conference to be encouraging, but nothing crazy happened to us that was much different from other church conference settings. But on the second day, that all changed. To my surprise, I was invited to join the leadership of the conference in the greenroom, where they shared lunch. I was seated next to modern-day prophet Kris Vallotton, and we entered into what became for me a mind-blowing conversation. For an hour, he told me things about my life he could not previously have known. Until that moment, we'd never met.

He later invited my two friends up to the greenroom and gathered a prophetic team around us to pray. Each of my friends experienced the same thing I had from Kris. Men and women interceded for us. They laid hands on us, listened for God's voice, and then imparted words to us as they sensed God was speaking. The moment was stunning. We wept with joy.

We sometimes hear of strange things happening to others, but when it happens to us specifically, it leaves us speechless, in awe of God. I'm grateful we have the written Bible. I trust every word. I'm also grateful that the God who spoke is still speaking. His speech today never contradicts what is written, but he does provide clarity and insight for each of us in unique ways both natural and supernatural.

This brings us to Anna, a prophetess at the time of Jesus's dedication at the temple. She knew the ancient Scriptures inside and out, and she also heard fresh insight from the Spirit of God. The Scriptures have spoken, and the Spirit is speaking:

> There was a prophetess, Anna, the daughter of Phanuel, of the tribe of Asher. (Luke 2:36, ESV)

WHAT IS A PROPHET(ESS)

A prophet(ess) is a revealer—one who provides insights into things past, present, and future based on God's revelation. Mature prophets provide specifically keen direction rather than general, vague observation. I also believe that a prophet's insight must be tested and not naively believed (see 1 Thessalonians 5:20–21).

Prophetic gifts are not an identity; rather, they are spiritual fruit born from life with God. Just like those people with the gift of teaching or administration, prophets are not to overidentify with their gift. Whereas the gifts of the Spirit are profound, they are merely extensions of intimacy with God.

In Luke 2, we meet Anna, an elderly prophetess. She was given divine revelation through the Spirit to approach Joseph and Mary with a word of knowledge about the significance of their child. Anna had spent decades devoted to worship, prayer, service, and study in the temple. You might think your grandma was a committed churchgoer, but she probably had nothing on Anna. Anna's dedication provided her clear prophetic insight. God gives wisdom to those he trusts, so when Jesus was brought forth for dedication, the Spirit immediately revealed the child's significance to Anna. The key principle for godly prophecy is always intimacy with God. Little intimacy, little insight. Great intimacy, great insight.

THE MEANING OF NAMES

In ancient times, names carried great significance. Luke tells us that Anna was the daughter of Phanuel and from a tribe of Israel called Asher. When unpacked, each of these names provides us a deeper understanding of the story.

Anna means "grace," or "favor." It is the Greek form of the Hebrew name Hannah. Anna derives her name from Hannah, the mother of Samuel. A thousand-ish years before Anna laid eyes on the baby who would lead Israel, Hannah brought her baby who would lead Israel to the house of the Lord at Shiloh. Anna's experience on the day Jesus was brought to the temple was God's pure grace, God's abundant favor. Anna's father's name, *Phanuel,* means "face of God." Phanuel's daughter would fulfill the meaning of his name. That day in the temple courts, Anna saw the face of God in the Christ child.

Asher, the tribe of Anna's family, means "happy." The tribe of Asher settled in the most northern part of Israel on the Mediterranean Sea. Scripture speaks of this tribe as being those who ate the richest of foods (see Genesis 49:20) and bathed in the finest of oil (see Deuteronomy 33:24). Their land was fertile and their path prosperous. However, the tribe of Asher was not obedient to fully driving out the Canaanites among them (see Judges 1:31–32). Over time, the tribe of Asher mixed cultures with Gentile Phoenicians (then later with the Seleucid Empire) and were then conquered by Pompey of Rome in 63 B.C. Although some of the people of Asher remained faithful to God, most of them were subject to despair and brokenness. Pompey is important to the story of Anna's journey to Jerusalem, as you will see in the next few paragraphs.

In some ways, Anna's life resembled the tribe Asher: a combination of blessed and broken. We are led to believe that after the death of her husband, she departed the territory of Asher, moving south to Jerusalem to worship and wait for the Lion of the tribe of Judah to appear. Let's dig deeper:

> She was very old; she had lived with her husband seven years after her marriage, and then was a widow until she was eighty-four. (Luke 2:36–37)

Luke informs his reader of many details while also leaving room for the imagination to wander. Applying some simple math, we discover a fascinating connection between Rome and Pompey, its leader at the time of Anna's upbringing. Like Mary, Anna, too, married around age fifteen and lived with her husband for seven years until his death. She was therefore around age twenty-two when widowed. Anna then went to live at the temple until age eighty-four, which means she had devoted about sixty years of her life to temple service. I wonder if she struggled to believe that God was good—that he would restore. I wouldn't blame her. After all, she was human.

> She never left the temple but worshiped night and day, fasting and praying. (verse 37)

I believe that one of the lessons we can learn from Anna's life is that after the death of her husband, Anna eventually ran toward and not away from God. Instead of running from community, she relocated to live in the center of the community of faith. Tempting as it might have been to stew in anger over the tragic circumstances of life, she expanded in hope, believing that the redemption of Jerusalem would come to make all things new.

Day and night, for sixty years, she worshipped, fasted, prayed, and studied. The Christian tradition would later refer to faithful women like Anna as "anchoress." These are women who anchor their lives in devotion to God through prayer, service, and worship. Can you imagine the spiritual depth and maturity of this woman on that day when Mary and Joseph ascended the steps and walked onto the Temple Mount with a baby in their arms?

Imagine also the clarity, insight, and faith she cultivated. Both Anna and Simeon were faithful God seekers in Jerusalem at the time Jesus was born. Their experience of great loss at the hand of Rome must have been significant. But they also must have used that hardship to press them deep into hope and not despair. *If we keep praying, watching, waiting, surely the redeemer of Jerusalem will arrive,* they must have thought often.

For some people, disappointment drives them away from God. Yet for others, it does just the opposite, driving them straight to his heart in hopes of deliverance and breakthrough:

> Coming up to them at that very moment, she gave thanks to God and spoke about the child to all who were looking forward to the redemption of Jerusalem. (verse 38)

What is meant by "all who were looking forward" is people of hope, faith, and expectation. The story of Scripture binds Anna's wounds from the past, calling her to look forward in hope, similar to Simeon. Anticipation grows expectation. Expectation is a good thing. Without it, we become bored and stale, going through the religious motions at best and walking away from faith at worst. But when expectations are attached to specific outcomes based on what and how we think events should unfold, expectation can quickly morph into control, breeding disappointment and cynicism when things don't turn out the way we imagined. We should expect. We should anticipate. But holding on to outcomes based on our preferred methods and timelines can be a mistake.

So, what exactly were Simeon and Anna expecting the

Messiah to do at that time? What precisely are we expecting the Messiah to do now in our time?

POLITICAL AND IMMEDIATE VERSUS SPIRITUAL AND PROCESS

When Anna looked for the redemption of Jerusalem, she sought liberation. In Hebrew, the word for "redemption" is *geulah,* which is fun to say when spoken from the gut. *Lutrosis* in Greek means "liberation," in the sense of freedom from oppression.[1] Jewish coins dating back to the Jewish Revolt (A.D. 66–70) read, "For the freedom [ge'ulah] of Jerusalem."[2] Anna's hope for redemption meant that Rome would not forever oppress God's people, yet Anna waited decades for God's deliverance. And when the deliverance came into the temple that day, it was still not immediate. She recognized deliverance in the form of a child who still had to grow up. And even after Jesus was fully grown, his deliverance was different than most expected.

Jesus is, indeed, a liberator, but he first aims to liberate us from our inner bondage. From that place of freedom, he calls us to join God in the work of seeking outer, societal liberation for others. Societal liberation is often slower than we prefer. God is more like a farmer than like a machinist. Jesus told many stories about seeds and soil, trees, and thistles. The kingdom is ultimate but not always immediate. Anna waited. Today we still wait. As we wait, God prunes, shapes, and forms us to become the solutions we long to see in the world. God wants a kind world, so he uses our life circumstances to make us kind. God wants a loving world, so he uses the relationships around us to form us into love. God wants a world of peace, so he calls us into silence and solitude each day so that peace can first be cultivated in us.

As God's kingdom takes shape in us over the years, we become the kinds of people who possess gifts that are helpful in the world. Our clarity improves, our wisdom grows, our prophetic words are precise, and our discernment is enhanced. Anna models this for us. A devout life grows in intimacy.

Reflection

Slowly read Luke 2:36–38, and then reflect on the sketch below. Ponder this question: What is my plan to increase my intimacy with God?

Epilogue

Practicing Christmas Today

This book began in Bethlehem. It seems fitting that it should end there as well. When in Bethlehem, it is important to visit one of the oldest churches in the world, called the Church of the Nativity. It was built over the top of where many people believe Jesus was born, although the accuracy of that claim is up for debate. What is not up for debate is the way in which an adult of average height enters the church.

Oddly, the door is only four feet in height and two feet in width. This feature today might fail a building inspection. The Ottomans built the door with a narrow width and low top to prevent cattle from entering. Now, let's think about this fact through a spiritual lens. The Church of the Nativity carries spiritual significance by the way a person must enter the door, referred to as "the door of humility."[1] It is impossible to gain access unless one is willing to bow low to enter. The inconvenience of the door reveals a core spiritual truth: Bowing down in humility is the gateway to spiritual wisdom and understanding.

The Christmas story is a humbling tale if there ever was one. How humiliating for God, in his first moment in the flesh, to be born in an area meant for animals and then to be immediately placed into a feeding trough to rest.

Our quest to unearth some of the hidden depths of the Advent story begins and ends with humility. There is always more to discover, and there is always more we will never fully know on this side of the new heaven and new earth. A small piece of advice for this time of year: It's one thing to know the story; it's another thing to let the story know you.

As we age—and, thus, hear the Christmas story year after year—we think we know it. And perhaps we do, on one level. But to truly *know* the story as God hopes is to humbly allow the story to find its way inside the deepest recesses of our hearts and "prepare him room" to explore our lives.

Mary and Joseph wrapped Jesus in swaddling clothes—something people did to lambs before the Passover—and placed him in a manger. Mangers were not often made of wood but rather were cut from stone. The second chapter of Luke says,

You will find a baby wrapped in cloths and lying in a manger. (verse 12)

It's curious, because the end of Luke says something similar:

Then he took it down, wrapped it in linen cloth and placed it in a tomb cut in the rock, one in which no one had yet been laid. (23:53)

Luke began and ended his gospel in what's called an *inclusio,* a technique (similar to bookends) authors use to make a point. And the point Luke made here was that there is nothing coincidental about the entire course of Jesus's life. From beginning to end, God was writing a poetic (and true) story. The baby will become the Lamb. The rock-made-manger that holds him from the start will be the same type of rock to house him in burial before his glorious resurrection. In the end, the child came to die. The bread was meant to be consumed. But the story—true as it is—does not end there. Alleluia! Come [again], Lord Jesus!

Acknowledgments

This book never would have come into existence without the help of some incredible people whose names are not on the cover. To them I express my deepest gratitude.

Thank you to editors Paul Pastor, with whom I began this project, and Susan Tjaden, who significantly partnered with me to bring this book into the world. I am also thankful for the entire WaterBrook team including Laura Wright, Cara Iverson, and so many more! Your work improved mine in every way.

Thank you to Jonathan Merritt, my agent and friend. Thank you to Eric Marshall and the musicians for *Young Oceans* for Christmas albums to inspire my writing in months not named December. Thank you to Jamie Lynch for a retreat space on a spectacular South Carolina farm. Thank you to Rod and Libby VanSolkema, Brad Gray, Brad Nelson, Marty Solomon, and Lois Tverberg, who helped me notice how context shapes everything. Thank you to my local church community for allowing me to test this material on you in sermon format.

Many thanks to artist, Rick Sargent. I am grateful for your friendship and your craft. Thank you for helping readers visualize the drama in each chapter.

Thank you to my daughter, Eloise, whose joyful wonder sparks new light in me around the season of Christmas and beyond. And thank you to Elaina—my spouse, my friend, my love, my life.

I am grateful most of all to Jesus, the Savior of the world. The whole story is about him. This I believe with everything in me: The story is true.

Notes

INTRODUCTION

1. See Nash Information Services, The Numbers, www.the
   -numbers.com/box-office-chart/daily/2017/12/25.
2. Emily Dickinson, *The Poems of Emily Dickinson: Reading
   Edition* (Cambridge, Mass.: Belknap / Harvard University
   Press, 1998), 163.

PART 1 | ADVENT: THE GIFT OF WAITING

1. Tish Harrison Warren, "Tish Harrison Warren on Advent,"
   The C4SO Podcast (Churches for the Sake of Others),
   November 29, 2022, https://c4so.org/podcast/tish-harrison
   -warren-on-advent.
2. Brian Zahnd, *The Anticipated Christ: A Journey Through
   Advent and Christmas* (St. Joseph, Mo.: Spello, 2022), 1.

CHAPTER 1 | MARY: PRESENCE

1. Kenneth E. Bailey, *Jesus Through Middle Eastern Eyes:
   Cultural Studies in the Gospels* (Downers Grove, Ill.:
   InterVarsity, 2008), 190.
2. Glen Scrivener, quoted in Rebecca McLaughlin, *Is Christmas
   Unbelievable? Four Questions Everyone Should Ask About the
   World's Most Famous Story* (Charlotte, N.C.: Good Book
   Company, 2021), 45.
3. Ben Myers, *The Apostles' Creed: A Guide to the Ancient Cate-
   chism,* Christian Essentials (Bellingham, Wash.: Lexham,
   2018), 24.
4. Stanley Hauerwas, *Matthew,* Brazos Theological Commen-
   tary on the Bible (Grand Rapids, Mich.: Brazos, 2006), 36.

5.   David Bivin, *New Light on the Difficult Words of Jesus: Insights from His Jewish Context,* ed. Lois Tverberg and Bruce Okkema (Holland, Mich.: En-Gedi Resource Center, 2005), 4.

6.   Rodrigo Pérez Ortega, " 'Breakthrough' Finding Shows How Modern Humans Grow More Brain Cells Than Neanderthals," Science.org, September 8, 2022, www.science.org /content/article/breakthrough-finding-shows-how-modern -humans-grow-more-brain-cells-neanderthals.

7.   Dallas Willard, *The Divine Conspiracy: Rediscovering Our Hidden Life in God* (San Francisco: Harper, 1998), 14.

8.   Willard, *Divine Conspiracy,* 14.

Chapter 2 | Joseph: Character

1.   E. Randolph Richards and Brandon J. O'Brien, *Misreading Scripture with Western Eyes: Removing Cultural Blinders to Better Understand the Bible* (Downers Grove, Ill.: InterVarsity, 2012), 97.

2.   John DeLancey, *Connecting the Dots Between the Bible and the Land of Israel* (Middletown, R.I.: Stone Tower, 2021), 423.

3.   *Father Stu,* directed by Rosalind Ross (Culver City, Calif.: Sony Pictures, 2022).

Chapter 3 | Innkeeper: Hospitality

1.   Kenneth E. Bailey, *Jesus Through Middle Eastern Eyes: Cultural Studies in the Gospels* (Downers Grove, Ill.: InterVarsity, 2008), 29.

2.   Henry Annesley Woodham, *Q. S. F. Tertulliani Liber Apologeticus: The Apology of Tertullian, with English Notes and a Preface* (Legare Street Press, 2022), 72.

Chapter 4 | Zechariah: Silence

1.   David Chapman and John D. Currid, *Archaeology Study Bible (English Standard Version)* (Wheaton, Ill.: Crossway, 2018), 1475.

2.   Joachin Jeremias, *Jerusalem in the Time of Jesus,* 3rd ed. with author's revisions to 1967 ed. (Philadelphia: Fortress, 1969), 104.

3. Jeremias, *Jerusalem in the Time of Jesus,* 199–200.

4. U2, "I Still Haven't Found What I'm Looking For," *The Joshua Tree,* Island Records, 1987.

5. Michael Patrick Barber, *The True Meaning of Christmas: The Birth of Jesus and the Origins of the Season* (San Francisco: Ignatius, 2021), 26.

6. Henri Nouwen, Campus Ministry Training, "Moving from Solitude to Community to Ministry," CS Media, www.csme dia1.com/jacobswellnj.org/solitude_community_ministry .pdf, 1.

7. St. Augustine, in *Ancient Christian Writers: On the Psalms, Vol. 1,* trans. Scholastica Hebgin and Felicitas Corrigan (Westminster, Md.: Newman, 1960), 297.

CHAPTER 5 | ELIZABETH: SOLITUDE

1. David Greene, "Do Those Birds Sound Louder to You? An Ornithologist Says You're Just Hearing Things," NPR, May 6, 2020, www.npr.org/sections/coronavirus-live-updates /2020/05/06/843271787/do-those-birds-sound-louder-to-you -an-ornithologist-says-youre-just-hearing-thin.

2. Kenneth E. Bailey, "Women in Ben Sirach and in the New Testament," in *For Me to Live: Essays in Honor of James Leon Kelso,* ed. Robert A. Coughenour (Cleveland: Dillon/ Leiderbach, 1972), 56–60.

3. Bailey, "Women in Ben Sirach," 56–60.

4. Kenneth E. Bailey, *Jesus Through Middle Eastern Eyes: Cultural Studies in the Gospels* (Downers Grove, Ill.: InterVarsity, 2008), 190, referencing Leonard Swidler, *Biblical Affirmations of Woman* (Philadelphia: Westminster, 1979), 150–59.

5. Bill Johnson, *Hosting the Presence: Unveiling Heaven's Agenda* (Shippensburg, Pa.: Destiny Image, 2012), 94.

CHAPTER 6 | JOHN THE BAPTIST: WONDER

1. Roger E. Olson, *Against Liberal Theology: Putting the Brakes on Progressive Christianity* (Grand Rapids, Mich.: Zondervan, 2022), 38.

2. Blaise Pascal, *Pensées,* Penguin Classics, trans. A. J. Krailsheimer (London: Penguin Group, 1995), 127–28.

3.   Lewis Carroll, *Through the Looking-Glass, and What Alice Found There* (New York: Macmillan, 1897), 100.

4.   Alister McGrath, in Matthew J. Franck, "Religion, Reason, and Same-Sex Marriage: Faulty Reasoning Behind the Claim That Opposition to Gay Marriage Is an Irrational Prejudice," *First Things,* May 2011, www.firstthings.com /article/2011/05/religion-reason-and-same-sex-marriage.

5.   Joel R. Beeke and Paul M. Smalley, "What the Name 'Jesus' Means for Believers," Crossway, November 4, 2020, www .crossway.org/articles/what-the-name-jesus-means-for -believers.

CHAPTER 7 | GABRIEL: NOTICING

1.   Charles Taylor, *A Secular Age* (Cambridge, Mass.: Belknap Press of Harvard University Press, 2018), 307.

2.   Brian Zahnd, *The Anticipated Christ: A Journey Through Advent and Christmas* (St. Joseph, Mo.: Spello, 2022), 122.

3.   Zahnd, *Anticipated Christ,* 122.

4.   Madeleine L'Engle, *Walking on Water: Reflections on Faith and Art* (New York: Convergent, 2016), 10.

5.   Louis Armstrong and Bob Thiele, "What a Wonderful World," Range Road Music Inc., 1967.

6.   L'Engle, *Walking on Water,* 10–11.

7.   "What If Wifi Was Visible?" YouTube video, 4:26, posted by "What If," December 10, 2019, www.youtube.com /watch?v=gYvKt0CT9bc.

8.   David Chapman and John D. Currid, *Archaeology Study Bible (English Standard Version)* (Wheaton, Ill.: Crossway, 2018), 1368.

PART 2 | CHRISTMAS: THE GIFT OF RECEIVING

1.   Clement C. Moore, *The Night Before Christmas: The Classic Edition* (Kennebunkport, Maine: Applesauce, 2011).

2.   Brian Zahnd, *The Anticipated Christ: A Journey Through Advent and Christmas* (St. Joseph, Mo.: Spello, 2022), 3.

3.   Michael Patrick Barber, *The True Meaning of Christmas:*

The Birth of Jesus and the Origins of the Season (San Francisco: Ignatius, 2021), 16.

4. Barber, *True Meaning of Christmas,* 168.

CHAPTER 8: SHEPHERDS: CHOSEN

1. Joachim Jeremias, *Jerusalem in the Time of Jesus,* 3rd ed. with author's revisions to 1967 ed. (Philadelphia: Fortress, 1969), 306.

2. Jeremias, *Jerusalem in the Time of Jesus,* 304.

3. Charles Haddon Spurgeon, "No Room for Christ in the Inn" (sermon, Metropolitan Tabernacle, Newington, London, December 21, 1862), www.spurgeon.org/resource-library/sermons/no-room-for-christ-in-the-inn/#flipbook.

CHAPTER 9 | MAGI: GENEROSITY

1. A reference to Gary Chapman, *The Five Love Languages: The Secret to Love That Lasts* (Woodmere, N.Y.: Northfield, 2015).

2. "Ridiculously Extravagant Celebrity Gift Exchanges," *Stars Insider,* June 28, 2023, www.starsinsider.com/celebrity/362370/ridiculously-extravagant-celebrity-gift-exchanges.

3. W. D. Davies and Dale C. Allison, Jr., *The Gospel According to Saint Matthew,* 3 vols. (London: T&T Clark International, 2004), 1:228.

4. Michael Patrick Barber, *The True Meaning of Christmas: The Birth of Jesus and the Origins of the Season* (San Francisco: Ignatius, 2021), 113.

5. Origen, *Contra Celsum* 1.60, trans. Henry Chadwick (Cambridge: Cambridge University Press, 1953), 54–55.

6. Lois Tverberg, *Reading the Bible with Rabbi Jesus: How a Jewish Perspective Can Transform Your Understanding* (Grand Rapids, Mich.: Baker Books, 2019), 51.

7. Kenneth E. Bailey, *Jesus Through Middle Eastern Eyes: Cultural Studies in the Gospels* (Downers Grove, Ill.: InterVarsity, 2008), 54.

8. Bailey, *Jesus Through Middle Eastern Eyes,* 52.

9. Bailey, *Jesus Through Middle Eastern Eyes,* 52.

10. Bailey, *Jesus Through Middle Eastern Eyes,* 54.

11. Fulton Sheen, in Robert Barron, "Five Lessons of the Magi," Appleseeds.org, January 6, 2002, www.appleseeds.org/5 _Lessons_Magi_Barron.htm.

12. Victor H. Matthews, "The Unwanted Gift: Implications of Obligatory Gift Giving in Ancient Israel," Gale Academic OneFile (Society of Biblical Literature, Summer 1999), https:// go.gale.com/ps/i.do?p=AONE&u=googlescholar&id=GALE %7CA78436326&v=2.1&it=r&sid=AONE&asid=0e71cc6e.

13. Robert Barron, Facebook, January 3, 2021, www.facebook .com/BishopRobertBarron/photos/a.343034215735712 /3721401384565628/?type=3.

14. *The Book of Common Prayer* (New York: Church Publishing Incorporated, 1979), 399.

15. Rebecca McLaughlin, *Is Christmas Unbelievable? Four Questions Everyone Should Ask About the World's Most Famous Story* (Charlotte, N.C.: Good Book Company, 2021), 20.

16. Bailey, *Jesus Through Middle Eastern Eyes,* 36.

17. Joseph Mohr and Franz Gruber, "Silent Night," 1833, public domain.

CHAPTER 10 | HEROD: DARKNESS

1. Kenneth E. Bailey, *Jesus Through Middle Eastern Eyes: Cultural Studies in the Gospels* (Downers Grove, Ill.: InterVarsity, 2008), 58, 62.

2. The Talmud, in Rabbi Dovid Rosenfeld, "Chapter 3, Mishna 15(b): Masking Holiness—Part II," Pirkei Avos, Torah.org, December 9, 2022, https://torah.org/learning /pirkei-avos-chapter3-15b.

CHAPTER 11 | CAESAR AUGUSTUS: AUTHORITY

1. Tiffany Means, "What Happens When Two Hurricanes Collide?," Treehugger, July 13, 2021, www.treehugger.com /what-happens-when-two-hurricanes-collide-5191063 #citation-3.

2. Mark Cartwright, "Circus Maximus," World History Encyclopedia, www.worldhistory.org/Circus_Maximus.

3. Nandini B. Pandey, "Caesar's Comet, the Julian Star, and the Invention of Augustus," *Transactions of the American Philological Association (1974–2014)* 143, no. 2 (Autumn 2013): 405–49, www.jstor.org/stable/43830268.

4. Virgil, *Aeneid, 6.780–793,* trans. H. Rushton Fairclough (New York: Putnam's Sons, 1922), 561.

5. *OGIS 2,* no. 458; ca. 9 B.C.

6. Horace, *Odes* 4.15; ca. 13 B.C.

7. MrMacSon, "The Priene [Calendar] Inscription," Biblical Criticism and History Forum, June 11, 2017, https://early writings.com/forum/viewtopic.php?t=3255.

8. Horace, *Odes* 4.15; ca. 13 B.C.

9. Yuval Noah Harari, *Sapiens: A Brief History of Humankind* (New York: Harper, 2015), 31.

10. Brad Nelson (Infusion Bible Conference, Church of the City, Franklin, Tennessee, 2021).

11. Rome gave us the word *civilization.* To be civilized was to no longer be a barbarian.

12. Randy Smith (Infusion Bible Conference, Church of the City, Franklin, Tennessee, 2021).

13. *OGIS 2,* no. 458; ca. 9 B.C., emphasis added.

14. Virgil, *Aeneid* 6.780–793, trans. H. Rushton Fairclough (New York: Putnam's Sons, 1922), 561.

15. Brad Nelson (Infusion Bible Conference, Church of the City, Franklin, Tennessee, 2021).

16. Brad Gray (Infusion Bible Conference, Church of the City, Franklin, Tennessee, 2021).

17. David Van Biema, "Jerusalem at the Time of Jesus," *Time,* April 16, 2001, https://content.time.com/time/world /article/0,8599,2047474-2,00.html.

18. Donald Trump, in Dan Roberts and Ben Jacobs, "Donald Trump Proclaims Himself 'Law and Order' Candidate at Republican Convention," *The Guardian,* July 22, 2016, www .theguardian.com/us-news/2016/jul/21/donald-trump -republican-national-convention-speech.

19. Hillary Clinton, in David Smith, "All Eyes Will Be on a Composed Hillary Clinton at the Inauguration That Got

Away," *The Guardian,* January 16, 2017, www.theguardian
.com/world/2017/jan/16/hillary-clinton-inauguration
-reaction.

20. Michael Patrick Barber, *The True Meaning of Christmas: The
    Birth of Jesus and the Origins of the Season* (San Francisco:
    Ignatius, 2021), 103.

CHAPTER 12 | SIMEON: EXPECTATION

1. Søren Kierkegaard, *Journalen* JJ:167 (1843), *Søren Kierke-
   gaards Skrifter,* Søren Kierkegaard Research Center, Copen-
   hagen, 1997—, 18:306.

2. "The History of Pidyon Haben," Chabad.org, www.chabad
   .org/library/article_cdo/aid/928156/jewish/The-History-of
   -Pidyon-Haben.htm.

CHAPTER 13 | ANNA: SCRIPTURE

1. Solomon Schechter and Lewis N. Dembitz, "Ge'ullah
   ('Redemption')," Jewish Encyclopedia, www.jewish
   encyclopedia.com/articles/6644-ge-ullah.

2. "'For the Freedom of Jerusalem': Ancient Coin Shows
   More Support for Revolt Than Known Before," The
   Tower, May 3, 2018, www.thetower.org/for-the-freedom
   -of-jerusalem-ancient-coin-shows-more-support-for-revolt
   -than-known-before.

EPILOGUE

1. Rev. Mark H. Creech, "America and 'The Door of Humility,'" The Christian Post, January 1, 2009, www.christian
   post.com/news/america-and-the-door-of-humility.html.

© SARAH L. KISTLER

AJ SHERRILL follows Jesus and lives with his wife, Elaina, and their daughter, Eloise. He pastors Saint Peter's Anglican Church near Charleston, South Carolina, and has a doctor of ministry degree from Fuller Seminary. In AJ's spare time, he enjoys reading books, writing books, and buying more books. He also likes basketball, despite his left knee's protest. You can find other books he's written and stuff he's up to at AJSherrill.org.